Enriching FEEDBACK
in the primary classroom

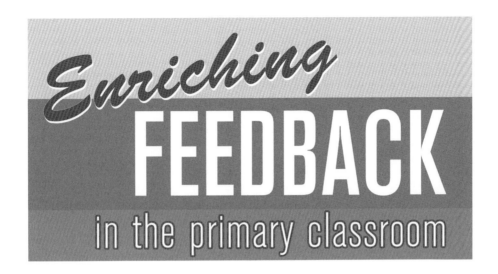

Enriching FEEDBACK in the primary classroom

Oral and written feedback from teachers and children

Shirley Clarke

Hodder Murray

A MEMBER OF THE HODDER HEADLINE GROUP

Orders: please contact Bookpoint Ltd, 130 Milton Park, Abingdon, Oxon OX14 4SB. Telephone: (44) 01235 827720. Fax: (44) 01235 400454. Lines are open from 9.00 to 6.00, Monday to Saturday, with a 24-hour message answering service. You can also order through our website www.hoddereducation.co.uk.

British Library Cataloguing in Publication Data
A catalogue record for this title is available from the British Library

ISBN-10: 0 340 87258 6
ISBN-13: 978 0 340 87258 1

First published 2003
Impression number   10   9   8   7   6   5
Year   2009   2008   2007   2006   2005

Hodder Headline's policy is to use papers that are natural, renewable and recyclable products and made from wood grown in sustainable forests. The logging and manufacturing processes are expected to conform to the environmental regulations of the country of origin.

Cover photo from Sally and Richard Greenhill.
Typeset by Servis Filmsetting Ltd, Manchester.
Printed in Great Britain for Hodder Education, a division of Hodder Headline, 338 Euston Road, London NW1 3BH, by Arrowsmith, Bristol.

Contents

Acknowledgements

I would like to thank the Gillingham Partnership Educational Action Zone – established under the Schools Standards and Framework Act 1998, by the Department for Education and Skills (DfES) to raise standards of education of groups of schools within socio-economically disadvantaged areas – for inviting me to carry out an exciting, large-scale formative assessment project. This book draws much of its content from the findings. There are too many teachers and administrators involved to name individuals, but I am indebted to the schools involved for allowing me to learn from their action research:

Arden Junior School, Medway
Barnsole Infant School, Medway
Barnsole Junior School, Medway
Brompton Westbrook Primary School, Medway
Byron Primary School, Medway
Featherby Infant School, Medway
Featherby Junior School, Medway
Hillyfields Junior School, Medway
Napier Primary School, Medway
Richmond Infant School, Medway
Saxon Way Primary School, Medway
Skinner Street Primary School, Medway
Twydall Infant School, Medway
Twydall Junior School, Medway
Upbury Manor Secondary School, Medway
Woodlands Primary School, Medway

As always, my work depends on the continued feedback from teachers and LEAs around the country and abroad. I would like to thank the following for their contributions to this book:

Carolyn Lyndsay, St Elizabeth School, Tower Hamlets
Fleetdown Infant School, Dartford, Kent
Ridgeway Primary School, Croydon
Suffolk LEA
Harrow LEA Project teachers
Southend LEA Project teachers
The Gillingham Learning Team
The children from Gillingham schools, who gave us so much information when interviewed and let us photocopy their work

Linda Sibbons, Leeds LEA
Michael Holmes

I would also like to thank the following people:

John Holmes, for everything
My parents and family, for their amazing support during
this year
Bet McCallum, for steering the Gillingham Project and for
her illuminating analysis
Chas Knight, for his usual editorial brilliance
Martin Garwood, Project Director of the Gillingham
Partnership, for the opportunities
Barry Silsby, for welcome comments on the manuscript
All the teachers who have attended my short and one-day
courses across the UK.

Shirley Clarke

Contacts:

www.shirleyclarke-education.org – for information about
various courses and for updates on Learning Team findings;
shirleyclarke@wi.rr.com – for feedback on teaching,
assessment and classroom issues arising from this book.

Photocopiable Resources

Photocopiable resources to support the use of this book for INSET are available on the *Enriching Feedback in the Primary Classroom* page of the Hodder website:

www.hodderheadline.co.uk

They can also be accessed on:

www.shirleyclarke-education.org

and via links on www.madaboutbooks.com and www.hoddertests.co.uk

Introduction

'In order for formative assessment to be embedded in practice, it is vital that teachers have children's learning as their priority, not their teaching or the opinions of outside parties.'

(Clarke, 2003)

Enriching Feedback in the Primary Classroom follows *Unlocking Formative Assessment* (Clarke, 2001) and *Targeting Assessment in the Primary Classroom* (Clarke, 1998). The previous books took all elements of formative assessment and discussed practical strategies for implementing the research principles. This book is intended to focus on perhaps the most powerful aspect of formative assessment: feedback.

I continue to work with teachers across the UK and increasingly abroad, to attempt to define ways in which formative assessment can be implemented successfully in the classroom, making sure that known research principles are adhered to. I encourage teachers to see themselves as action researchers when they are experimenting with their own and other teachers' ideas, as equal learners with the children. Keeping notes of approaches that worked, and interesting findings, are encouraged, so that quality discussions can take place outside the classroom when teachers come together.

The most comprehensive study I was involved in recently was with the *Gillingham Partnership* (The North Gillingham Education Action Zone) throughout 2001, in which 15 primary schools engaged in formative assessment over the course of a year: all teachers and all children, with teams of researchers interviewing teachers and children each term and observing lessons. A great deal was learnt during this time, most of all from the interviews with children. A core team of teachers continues to meet and their work, the results of the original study and the work of many other teams of teachers around the UK are reflected throughout this book.

Formative assessment

'
Formative assessment consists of the following components:

■ *The active involvement of pupils in their own learning;*

■ *Sharing learning goals with pupils;*

■ *Involving pupils in self-assessment;*

■ *Effective questioning;*

■ *Providing feedback which leads to pupils recognising their next steps and how to take them;*

■ *Adjusting teaching to take account of the results of assessment;*

■ *Confidence that every student can improve (the 'untapped potential' rather than 'fixed IQ' belief).* '

(Black and Wiliam, 1998)

Black and Wiliam's (1998) review of the literature about formative assessment proved that formative assessment raises standards of achievement and equips children for life-long learning.

In order for formative assessment to be embedded in practice, it is vital that teachers have *children's learning* as their priority: not their teaching or the opinions of outside parties. This is easy to say, but less easy to implement. This book takes account of the realities of the classroom and external pressures, within the context of striving for a whole-school rationale. Ways of facilitating and nurturing children's learning and their desire to learn override all other aims. Teaching is, of course, a key instrument, and throughout the book strategies are shared and analysed so that the best of practice can 'travel'.

Formative assessment is a powerful vehicle for focusing on effective learning. However, it is not a quick fix: it takes time, thought and discussion to become embedded. It also involves, in many cases, a gradual power shift, through modelling and training, enabling children to gradually take more and more control over their learning and the decisions they make to enhance that learning. Askew and Lodge's (2000) framework for feedback encapsulates the entire learning journey from teachers' control to pupil power:

Learning style	View of feedback
Instruction (*direct teaching*)	The Gift
Construction (*dialogue between teacher and child*)	Ping-pong
Co-construction (*free-flow dialogue between teachers and children separately and together*)	Loops

(Askew and Lodge, 2000)

We are aiming for 'loops', but we may need to include more 'gifts' and 'ping-pong' at the beginning of the continuum of control in order to reach that point.

The same principles and continuum must be necessary when working with adults in their professional development. Formative assessment only works when teachers come to own it for themselves – when they can talk to others about the way it works in their classroom, and when they become part of the huge number of teachers continually discovering and understanding better ways of helping children not only to learn but to love learning.

Feedback

Feedback is the central theme of formative assessment, yet is the element most laden with a legacy of bad practice and misguided views. We have tended, through various forms of feedback, to compare children constantly, thus demoralising the less able and making complacent the more able. We have focused feedback on limited features and often made children lose self-esteem and motivation. Parental expectations compound the problem.

Feedback issues covered in this book span feedback from teacher to child, from children to teacher, and to other children, in oral, written and some more subtle forms. The scene is set with some discussion about learning theories.

The foundations of feedback are laid through the chapters on devising and sharing learning intentions and developing success criteria. Various aspects of feedback are then explored in practical contexts, including whole-school issues about a feedback policy and framework. At the end of each chapter, the key principles are summarised and ideas are given for INSET.

1 Creating a learning culture in which effective feedback can exist

'If pupils don't learn the way we teach ... perhaps we should teach the way they learn.'

(Eppig, 1981)

In order for formative assessment to take place, and for feedback to be useful and based on multiple communications, we need to be clear about our aims for children's learning – not just *what* we want them to learn, but *how* we want them to learn, so that they leave school with the desire to learn and with enough knowledge about how to do this if left to their own devices. This, of course, means we also have to look at how we are teaching.

The search for answers about how children learn and how teachers need to teach is never-ending, and the main source of answers is teachers' own findings. The following section outlines the most significant theories about learning and teaching which we need to pay attention to when considering formative assessment and effective feedback.

The constructivist classroom

Formative assessment is increasingly linked with the **constructivist** model, in which the *learner* is responsible for the learning and the construction of knowledge, through cooperative situations, open-ended questioning, discussion and discovery learning set in meaningful contexts.

‘ *The most important single factor influencing learning is what the learner already knows. Ascertain this and teach him accordingly.* ’

(Ausubel et al., 1978)

Although it would seem obvious that teachers should create learning environments which follow these sentiments, some teachers resist the constructivist approach – because they are embedded in their old way of teaching, they don't believe it will make children learn better, they are satisfied with their students' grades and want no more for them, or they are worried that they will somehow lose control if children are given more stake in their learning. The constructivist classroom does involve the teacher in taking risks and systematically relinquishing control. Ironically, though, rather than losing control, the teacher gains more satisfaction and finds herself in a classroom in which children are better behaved and more motivated to learn. Once children understand their true place as learners, with the teacher as a facilitator, they let go of the struggle to conform to the teacher's wishes and do what she wants them to do and focus instead on finding the best ways of learning. In these circumstances, they expect the teacher and others to help them learn.

The characteristics of a constructivist classroom inevitably include the use of formative assessment. Brooks and Brooks (1993) list twelve descriptors of constructivist teaching behaviours, which should be helpful in clarifying the constructivist approach. I provide some interpretation in italics.

1 Constructivist teachers encourage and accept student autonomy and initiative – *pupils frame their own questions and find answers.*

2 Constructivist teachers use raw data and primary sources, along with manipulative, interactive and physical materials – *pupils look for evidence rather than receiving knowledge passively and link concepts to real-life situations, events and objects.*

3 When framing tasks, constructivist teachers use cognitive terminology such as 'classify', 'analyse', 'predict' and 'create' – *teachers go beyond literal questions of how, what and who, thus encouraging higher-level thinking.*

4   Constructivist teachers allow student responses to drive lessons, shift instructional strategies and alter content – *the curriculum determines what must be taught, not how ... whether the learning intention is being met or not is the prime concern – lesson content should change to best facilitate pupil learning.*

5   Constructivist teachers inquire about students' understandings of concepts before sharing their own understanding of these concepts – *concept mapping or brainstorming before unit planning takes place ensures that the teacher takes account of the children's current understandings and interests.*

6   Constructivist teachers encourage students to engage in dialogue, both with the teacher and with one another – *pupils are encouraged to present their own ideas as well as being permitted to hear and reflect on the ideas of others; paired two-minute discussions before general feedback leads to more powerful construction of new understandings or reflection of old ones.*

7   Constructivist teachers encourage student enquiry by asking thoughtful, open-ended questions and encouraging students to ask questions of each other – *teachers use Bloom's hierarchy of questions: literal questions, application questions, analytical questions, questions requiring synthesis and evaluation questions.*

8   Constructivist teachers seek elaboration of students' initial responses – *by using a multiple choice approach: 'What exactly do you mean? Do you mean this ..., do you mean that ..., or do you have an idea of your own?' and delving. Modelling possible pupil responses gives children a way in: 'I think your answer to this might be ... or ... What do you think?'*

9   Constructivist teachers engage students in experiences that might engender contradictions to their initial hypotheses and then encourage discussion – *teachers ask questions which set up contradictions to encourage discussion: e.g. 'So it is wrong to steal. But would it still be wrong to rob a bank if your children were starving?'*

10   Constructivist teachers allow wait time after posing questions – *children need approximately five seconds after the question is asked. Some teachers tell children not to put hands up until the end of the five seconds. Some ask for no hands up at all, so all have a chance of being asked.*

11   Constructivist teachers provide time for students to construct relationships and create metaphors – *asking 'what if?' questions to encourage links between ideas and giving children time to create metaphors for their understandings.*

12   Constructivist teachers nurture students' natural curiosity through frequent use of the learning cycle model – *(i) children interact with selected materials and generate questions and hypotheses; (ii) teacher focuses the children's questions as a way of introducing the concept; (iii) children work on new problems as a way of applying the concept.* **'**

Multiple intelligences and research about the brain

Howard Gardner (1983) introduced the idea, based on research about different abilities being located in different parts of the brain, that we have several different types of intelligences:

■ Linguistic intelligence

■ Logical or mathematical intelligence

■ Musical intelligence

■ Spatial and visual intelligence

■ Kinaesthetic intelligence

■ Interpersonal intelligence

■ Intrapersonal intelligence

Some people argue that there are other types of intelligence missing from this list, such as *common sense intelligence, naturalist intelligence* (the ability to work with nature) and *emotional intelligence,* as well as perhaps the most important 'intelligence' – the ability to create totally new concepts by *linking together existing concepts.*

The implications of these ideas are that we need to be considering children's preferred learning styles, motivations and natural tendencies, and that each person has a range of abilities which should be nourished and expressed throughout their education.

We need to structure learning in ways which are compatible with the way the brain learns naturally:

'
- *when it is trying to make sense;*
- *when it is building on what it already knows;*
- *when it recognises the significance of what it is doing;*
- *when it is working in complex, multiple perspectives;*
- *when it is learning collaboratively in a social/team setting.* '

(Abbott, 1994)

The intelligences do not operate in isolation for any of us, nor do they develop at the same rate. Many children (and adults) believe that they lack cognitive ability in any subject at which they are slower than their peers. For some aspects of their learning, people often need more time, input and especially effort to be applied. The number of driving tests needed before a recognised acceptable standard is reached varies from person to person: one example of how people need more time and input for some aspects of learning than others. Unlike school subjects, however, we are highly motivated to learn to drive, so we persevere and put in extra time and effort to succeed. If only this motivation could be transferred to the classroom! Unfortunately, children quickly decide that they lack ability when constantly compared to other children in the class by explicit or implicit means or when their particular strengths are not valued.

Motivation and self-esteem

How children perceive themselves and their ability is central to the success of the learning environment. Unless we pay attention to the factors that increase or decrease children's self-esteem and motivation, we are often working fruitlessly.

The recognised vital ingredients of self-esteem (Youngs, in Dryden and Vos, 2001) are:

■ Physical safety *(freedom from physical harm)*

■ Emotional safety *(the absence of intimidation and fears)*

■ Identity *(I am proud of being who I am)*

■ Affiliation *(a sense of belonging)*

■ Competence *(I can do this to the best of my ability)*

■ Mission *(my life has meaning and direction)*

Identity and Competence are also known as *self-worth* and *self-efficacy,* respectively. People often have a high sense of self-worth yet a low sense of self-efficacy (*I'm a nice person but I'm no good at anything*), or vice-versa (*I'm quite clever but people don't really like me*). Children's self-worth is developed mainly within their home situation, whereas their sense of self-efficacy can be greatly influenced by their educational experiences.

Learning from Japan

The Japanese culture emphasises the importance of *effort.* This focuses children on learning rather than competition and performance. Children receive as many congratulations for effort and perseverance as for academic achievement. They stay motivated for long periods of time because they know everyone believes the learning is possible for them, although it may take some time and effort.

Two books which have inspired me most in recent years are *The Learning Gap* (Stevenson and Stigler, 1992) and *The Teaching Gap* (Stigler and Hiebert, 1999). They compare American classrooms with Japanese classrooms and examine both cultures in depth. Thousands of hours of video were studied to come up with the findings. Some of the stark differences reported between US and Japanese methods, bearing in mind that lessons were generalised, are relevant for the UK classroom and other Western settings. My main point here is how the Japanese model promotes a high level of motivation, both for children and teachers, because there is a different way of seeing the role of the educator and the child as a learner compared to the traditional Western view. Some examples of the differences are given in the table.

US lessons	Japanese lessons
US teachers see mixed-ability groupings as a problem.	Japanese teachers see mixed ability as a gift: individual differences are seen as beneficial for the class because they produce a range of ideas, methods and solutions that provide the material for pupils' discussion and reflection.
US teachers differentiate by ability.	Japanese teachers see this as unfairly limiting and as prejudging what students are capable of learning: all students should have the opportunity to learn the same material.
US teachers hold students' attention by increasing pace, by praising work and behaviour, by having real-life tasks and by their own enthusiasm, humour and 'coolness'.	Japanese teachers believe that the learning itself is the greatest motivational tool.
US teachers tend to use an overhead projector for teaching points, turning it off when they want students to listen or work – they see it as an attentional and motivational tool.	Japanese teachers use a chalkboard/whiteboard as a continuous record of a lesson, which students have constant access to.
US pupils sit for many hours without a break.	School days are longer but each lesson is followed by a short playground break.
Most US lessons are continually interrupted.	Japanese lessons are never interrupted – the lesson is seen as sacrosanct.

The team also discovered many cultural differences that are impossible to replicate, like parental attitude to education (e.g. in Japan even the poorest homes have a desk for each child, whereas in American homes the adults' needs take priority). Interestingly, the authors dispel the myth that the Japanese system of education involves excessive pressures. They claim that, although parental pressure builds during the high school years, when concerns about university exams intensify, such pressure is not evident in pre-school or elementary school settings. Parents in Japan intensify their interest in their children's academic achievement as the children get older, with an expectation that the pre-school years should be confined to play and the development of social skills. American parents apply pressure to their children from the beginning, generally losing their interest as children grow older, believing that the school should become more responsible for pupil achievement. The authors also found that the idea that teaching methods in Japan stress rote learning is inaccurate. The parallels with the UK educational classroom are clear. We cannot simply tweak the existing culture in order to make learning the priority – we have to create institutions which have different ways of valuing learning.

What do we do to make things worse?

Many of the educational classroom experiences of the Western culture make learning difficult for children. Ken Robinson (2000) said *'It takes a lot of people of lot of time to recover from their education'*. This certainly resonates with me as it will with many teachers – who are probably in the top few per cent of high achievers in the country. How must the others feel?! I have memories of leaving primary school with a great deal of confidence in my ability and by the end of my first year at grammar school deciding that I was decidedly lacking. The teachers found my curiosity and need to ask lots of questions irritating. There was only one teaching style: reading from files while we took rapid notes, which were written up for homework and then learnt off by heart for an end-of-year test. Shorthand would have been invaluable! At the end of the first year, the top 30 girls (according to the test results) became the 'Latin' form, while the rest of us chose German or Spanish. I knew from that moment that I had failed. It was only much later, when I encountered apparent success at teaching, that I began to believe in my ability again. Such explicit comparisons of apparent ability are made in UK and Western classrooms all the time, which make children lose motivation in applying any kind of effort to their work.

In *Unlocking Formative Assessment*, I outline many factors which cause children to view themselves and their ability, and therefore their subsequent motivation, either with complacency or demoralisation. Those points are summarised:

1   External rewards (stickers, merit marks, etc) act like grades – treating every piece of work as a test freezes children into complacency or demoralisation. Children need feedback which is linked to the learning criteria of the task. The reward should be the celebration of the learning achieved or the effort expended.

2   We need to analyse our body language, tone of voice and phrasing in the classroom when interacting with individuals. These are powerful 'give-aways' to children about how the teacher perceives them.

3   We need to review the use of classroom assistants in the classroom: do they automatically sit with the same children, giving a clear message that they will be unable to do the work without help?

4   We need to review our use of withdrawal groups and setting. Children can be given different work yet not have to move rooms. Differentiation by outcome is more enabling than differentiation by task. Children know the hierarchy within the classroom – why rub their noses in it?

5   We need to change the way in which children perceive difficulty as failure. Challenge is an exciting indication of new learning. Say *'I'm pleased that this is making you think. It means you are learning something new. If you already knew how to do it, there would be no new learning!'*

6   Use praise sparingly. Offer congratulations after asking the child to comment on the best aspect of their work first, so they take the lead and avoid becoming 'praise junkies'.

Carol Dweck's (1986) work on motivation summarises what happens if you get children to focus on competitive structures (*performance orientation*) rather than on what they have learnt and what they need to do to improve (*learning orientation*):

Performance orientation (*I want the best grade/a sticker/* *to be first*)	Learning orientation (*I want to work hard/I want to* *learn and know how to improve*)
Belief that ability leads to success.	Belief that effort leads to success.
Concern to be judged as able and to perform.	Belief in one's ability to improve and learn.
Satisfaction from doing better than others or succeeding with little effort.	Derives satisfaction from personal success at difficult tasks.
Emphasis on interpersonal competition and public evaluation.	Applies problem solving and self-instructions when engaged in tasks.
Helplessness: evaluates self negatively when task is difficult.	

The social context of learning

Finally, we need to think not only about the learning, but the situation in which the learning takes place and the influence of those factors in promoting or demoting motivation and effective learning.

Vygotsky (1978) established the *zone of proximal development* as the challenge factor in learning – the difference between what children can do independently and what they can accomplish with the support of others. The constructivist model promotes cooperative situations as essential for effective learning, with much classroom talk – between children and teachers and between children together. In the first term of the Gillingham Project, representatives from two of the schools said that teachers were already noticing that children were able to write more, across the subjects. The teachers attributed this to the fact that pupils were now involved in more 'learning talk' at the beginnings and ends of lessons (sharing learning intentions, developing success criteria and self-evaluating).

It is through group discussions and cooperative learning situations that trust develops, which in itself motivates and makes secure the learning context for the child. As Abrami et al. (1995) say: *'Co-operation promotes trust, trust promotes co-operation, greater co-operation results in greater trust.'*

So...

It is essential that all teachers within a school develop a teaching and learning policy together, to be committed to their beliefs and ideals for their pupils and their school. Without this, any departure into the world of formative assessment will be fraught with problems. Teachers who are not natural constructivists will pay lip service to the ideas involved in formative assessment, but behind closed doors will carry on with their usual practice. Teachers who are instinctive constructivists, on the other hand, will read about formative assessment, and the rest of this book, and recognise much of their existing practice already. It is on that practice that we need to build, in order to achieve a universal school learning culture.

Key principles

- Formative assessment depends on a constructivist classroom.
- We need to plan for different intelligences and styles of learning.
- Effort should be applauded as much as achievement.
- Many traditions of Western education lower children's self-efficacy.
- We should focus children on a learning orientation rather than a performance orientation.

■ The social context plays a powerful part in motivation and the effectiveness of learning.

■ Schools need to have a well-discussed and agreed teaching and learning policy to underpin any work on formative assessment.

INSET ideas

1. Use the twelve descriptors of constructivist teaching behaviour in a staff meeting, having circulated them in advance. Get teachers in groups to take two or three of the points: discuss and come up with some practical examples. Feed back the examples to each other and have a general discussion about the implications for practice and for any change that might be required.

2. Look at Howard Gardner's descriptions of the different intelligences and discuss in a staff meeting.
   (a) Decide alone and then in pairs on own preferred learning orientations.
   (b) Use short-term plans to analyse a day's lessons: which intelligences do they favour? How can we strike a better balance?

3. Ask teachers to experiment for one week in the classroom, making a big deal about the amount of effort applied, whether the outcome is poor or excellent. In a subsequent staff meeting, feed back the impact on children's attitude to learning and their self-esteem.

4. Discuss use of classroom assistants, including them in this discussion, and decide on some more flexible patterns.

5. Get teachers to experiment with asking children to say what they like most about their work, before offering praise. Give feedback about the impact.

2 Learning intentions

'We have got to do a lot fewer things in school. The greatest enemy of understanding is coverage. As long as you are determined to cover everything, you actually ensure that most kids are not going to understand. You've got to take enough time to get kids deeply involved in something so they can think about it in lots of different ways and apply it – not just at school, but at home and on the street and so on.'

(Gardner, 1993)

Feedback – whether teacher to child, child to teacher, or child to child – needs to be based on clear understandings about the learning objective of the task and related success criteria. For this reason, the next two chapters focus specifically, and in great depth, on getting learning intentions and success criteria right at the planning stage and during lessons.

The coverage dilemma

One of the most problematic issues for a teacher today is knowing how to cover everything required by the curriculum while still engaging children in meaningful learning. There seems to be a pressure on teachers to have covered everything, yet, ironically, Office for Standards in Education (OFSTED) inspectors focus first and foremost on the quality of the learning experience for the child. It is generally true that the more covered, the less learnt. As Black and Wiliam (1998) said:

‘ *Teachers have to take risks in the belief that investment of time in formative assessment will reap rewards in the future, whilst 'delivery' and 'coverage' with poor understanding are pointless and even harmful.* ’

The following strategies for coping with the overloaded curriculum have proved to be useful:

1   Don't spend too much time on 'knowledge' learning intentions. Knowledge that is not being used is easily forgotten. No matter how interesting our lessons, we will not be able to ensure that knowledge will be remembered. Would anyone really know if you didn't teach it? It seems prudent, therefore, to spend limited time giving children knowledge information and spending more classroom time on skills and concepts in which the knowledge is *used*: information retrieval, designing experiments, writing accounts, drawing diagrams, and so on. After the knowledge is forgotten, the skills and concepts will remain. Strategies for imparting knowledge include giving information sheets, running quick overview lessons and use of multi media.

2   Decide which learning intentions in a long list to be covered are most significant, taking account of the previous point. Relinquish those learning intentions that will be revisited, will be learnt through natural life experiences or are small and trivial knowledge points.

3   Pass on 'key objective' sheets to the next teacher, highlighting in different colours those statements that most of the class have learnt, those that about half have learnt, and those that a quarter or less have learnt. This will help the next teacher to determine what most time should be spent on.

4   Capitalise on cross-curricular learning by writing on the short-term plan other learning intentions which will clearly be covered in this lesson, highlighting the one which will be the focus of the lesson. This provides 'evidence' of implicit rather than explicit coverage. The learning intention of the lesson remains the key focus for teaching, learning and feedback, but it is recognised that other learning is inevitable.

5   Don't get children to do endless exercises of sums or sentences which take up valuable learning time. Do two or three examples only, then go through these with the class. More will be learnt and less time will be spent.

6   Cut down on children's recording time in a lesson (see Chapter 3 for more about this).

7   Create a whole-school rationale to show that your priority is to achieve maximum learning rather than maximum coverage. Lengths of units in long-term plans can remain the same, but teachers should be able to follow the points above in deciding how best to facilitate learning within that timeframe. Write your agreed principles in a teaching and learning policy and stand firm when challenged. When there is a whole-school rationale for something and everyone is following the same course of action, and that can be justified, it is difficult for anyone to criticise – unless, of course, the test scores are repeatedly low, in which case all of the school's practice will be under criticism.

New ways of thinking about learning intentions: the penny drops!

Since the introduction of the National Curriculum there has really only been one way of thinking about learning intentions: *skills, concepts* and *knowledge*. In working with a 'learning team' of teachers in one London borough recently (teachers who meet me three times a year to feed back their action research on formative assessment), we discovered together that there appear to be actually only two kinds of learning intentions:

■ the *'bits'* that need to be specifically taught and learnt (skills, concepts and knowledge);

■ *applications* of those 'bits'.

For example:

'Bits' learning intentions (skills, concepts or knowledge)	Application learning intentions
English: To create a story opening in which dialogue is used.	**English:** To write a complete story.
Mathematics: To use repeated addition to solve division problems.	**Mathematics:** To solve division problems using any method.
Science: To know how to conduct a fair test.	**Science:** To be able to design and write up an experiment correctly.

This framework eliminates some ongoing problem issues. First, for many years teachers have been telling me that it is difficult to make *all* learning intentions specific and precise. This model explains why: *application* learning intentions are necessarily broad. Second, there are profound implications for the way we should plan over time. It is clear that we need a balance between the two types of lessons all the time – planning 'bits' lessons punctuated by 'application' lessons. But *why* is it important for teachers to plan regular 'application' lessons, before children have been 'taught' all the component parts required? Or, to put it another way, why is it important for children to write a whole story when they've only been taught to do specific openings? Why is it important to get children to design an experiment before they have learnt how to create a fair test?

Because...

■ You find out what they already know that hasn't yet been taught.

■ You find out whether they really know what you have taught – can they apply it in this context?

■ It gives them the whole picture, therefore making connections easier and providing purpose.

■ It gives them the whole picture, therefore providing motivation and interest.

■ Things go wrong (e.g. the science experiment doesn't work) and children can identify the need for the next 'bit' to be taught – *'We need to put the plants all in the same place next time!'*

■ You find out children's target needs (this child really needs some help on better story endings) and sometimes all children's needs (they all need help with story endings!).

Summative assessment of 'bits' is unreliable, because children appear to know it at the time. Applications are the only valid contexts. Focusing on success and improvement for 'bits' will develop those skills as far as possible: this is formative assessment in action!

When I started teaching, most lessons were of the 'application' type, with very little specific teaching of skills, apart from perhaps in mathematics. I believe that the situation has now reversed, so that the curriculum is dominated by 'bits' – lesson after lesson of all the specific skills, concepts and knowledge. Educational reform usually results in extreme swings, when what is really needed is a balance between the two approaches. The best scenario, taking account of the previous points, would probably be application–bits–application, in order to take account of prior learning and maximum motivation.

Other links: implications of the model for success criteria and feedback

Success criteria

The next chapter looks at success criteria in depth, but, in general terms, success criteria for specific skills, concepts and knowledge tend to be easy-to-create, step-by-step points which ensure a high level of success. On the other hand, success criteria for 'application' learning intentions tend to consist of all the things learnt so far about that application (e.g. when writing a whole story, remember to have a good opening, middle, ending, characterisation, good adjectives, etc). In other words, what was once a 'bit' now becomes a success criterion when used for an 'application' learning intention.

Feedback

Many teachers remark – and research shows – that, for most lessons, instant feedback seems more appropriate than reflective feedback. Specific skills, knowledge or concepts need instant feedback during lessons, or children can reach the end of a lesson feeling frustrated and having wasted learning time. The end of an art lesson is too late to tell the child they should have used less water when mixing colours. 'Application' learning intentions, on the other hand, lend themselves to more considered reflective feedback, on the part of both the child and the teacher. Ways forward for 'bits' are likely to be 'there and then', whereas 'application' targets will need to be applied over time.

This model has changed the way in which I 'see' learning intentions and success criteria, and I believe it provides a powerful framework within which to plan and operate during lessons. 'Bits' and 'applications' are explored in relation to success criteria in Chapter 3.

Getting learning intentions right at the planning stage: separating the learning intention from the context of the lesson

Over the last few years, I have noticed that many problems occur if the learning intention of the task is 'muddled' with the activity or context. For example *'To make a list of what a pet needs'* is a literacy learning intention muddled up with its context. The learning intention should, of course, read

'To be able to make a list.'

With the learning intention *'To list what a pet needs'*, the children are likely to be more focused on the pet than on the list-making, because a concrete context is more tangible than an abstract learning intention. The teacher is also more likely to be focused on the pet than the list-making and there is a good chance that some of the children will believe that a list is something you only make about pets. Thus the connections are not made.

I am suggesting that we need explicitly to separate the learning intention from its context, illustrating that there are many things we could choose as a vehicle for learning. For example: *'Today we are going to learn to be able to make a list. We could make a list of lots of different things – like what clothes we are wearing, books we have read…. What other things could we make a list of?'* With this approach, children are likely to see that there is a core skill which can be applied to many different things. The children and the teacher's focus is now firmly fixed on the list-making.

A geography learning intention for ten-year-olds illustrates the same muddle: **'To understand the effect of banana production on the banana producers'**. Children are likely to believe they are learning about bananas rather than production and almost certainly will think this is something which relates only to the production of bananas. The learning intention should read:

'To understand the effect of production on the producers.'

By clarifying the learning intention and the 'how' as bananas, children are shown explicitly that there are many different products to which this learning intention applies. Not only is the teacher's feedback likely to be more clearly focused on the learning intention rather than the context, she is likely to structure the lesson differently. It would seem appropriate, for instance, during the plenary to brainstorm the effect of production on the producers for other food products.

The two learning intentions used so far to illustrate this point are *skills* (to be able to…) and *concepts* (to understand…). These types of learning intentions suffer most frequently from the muddling effect. The third main type of learning intention, *knowledge* (to know…), is somewhat different. The context within a knowledge learning intention is important and not randomly chosen, as in the previous examples. For instance:

'To know the impact of Henry VIII's reign on the lives of ordinary people.'
'To know the names of parts of a plant.'

It is still important to explain to children that there are two elements to the learning intention (i.e. the impact of his life on people and the significance of the man himself), but the point can be made that the focus or context (i.e. Henry VIII/the plant) is deliberate, because of its importance.

Some examples of Literacy learning intentions 'before' and 'after':

Before ...	After ...	
Learning intention muddled with context	Learning intention	Context
To be able to write a version of Little Red Riding Hood.	To be able to write a version of a traditional text.	Little Red Riding Hood.
Write a short account about how you kept occupied on a journey.	To be able to write a short account with reasons.	Select items to keep you occupied on a long journey.
Describe a friend.	To be able to create an effective characterisation.	Describe a friend.

Sharing learning intentions with children during lessons – the big picture

It is very common now for teachers in UK schools to share learning objectives with children at the beginnings of lessons. However, I wonder if, for many children, their school world now consists of a conveyor belt of learning intentions, one lesson after another, with no coherent framework to link them meaningfully together. While they might be clear about the meaning and even the point of individual lessons, do they understand where the learning is going? And what sense can they make of so many separate lessons?

Some strategies for helping children make connections and see the overall learning plan

What do they already know?

A common starting point is to brainstorm with children before a unit of work begins what they already know about this topic and what they would like to know and learn about. Concept mapping and mind maps are often used as devices to help children put together their initial thoughts.

Schemes of work exist which mean that many learning intentions are already laid down. Perhaps a way forward here would be to list the learning intentions to be covered or show the main elements of the content to be covered (e.g. body parts, senses, keeping healthy) and find out from children at that point what they already know about these things and what they would still like to know. One teacher from one of my LEA learning teams described how she displays the learning intentions for a unit of work as questions, inviting children, through the course of the work, to write their own questions on the list.

Making connections

As a way of making connections clearer for children, start units by using a flipchart page of all the learning intentions – in full, as notes or as questions – to be covered over the period. It seems best to keep 'child speaking' to a minimum. Technical words are better kept intact: it is more muddling to try to rephrase specific terms, and children have a natural fascination with and aptitude for new words. The teacher takes the children through the 'big picture' by reading through the learning intentions. She then encourages them to say what they think these things will entail, and have a stab at interpreting some of the new terms.

Mind-mapping is a common tool at this point. In 'picture dictation', used in New Zealand, children are each given a key word from the coverage on a card, and asked to find out as much as they can about it, through research or discussion. They create a 'physical' mind-map with the cards, before a whole-class written version is created. Links and connections are made, and modified as the topic unfolds. As learning intentions are introduced, they are highlighted on the flipchart, and the whole thing is constantly referred to at the beginning and end of the associated lessons. For example, the following was displayed as an A3 poster throughout a Science topic at Year 2:

OURSELVES
       Body parts
       Senses
       Keeping healthy
                   – keeping clean
                   – taking exercise
                   – balanced diet

The visual image – having the learning words displayed – is vital for all learners in keeping the learning at the forefront. Such lists help children make important connections between concepts and skills and in their whole understanding of concepts and how to apply them to different situations, as well as keeping a mental track of what has been learnt and how it fits with the big picture.

Sharing learning intentions with children during lessons – using characters and acronyms

Lessons usually begin with the learning intention being introduced. The 'teaching' section follows, then a task and finally some kind of plenary. The success criteria are best drawn from the children just before the task. Over the last five years, teachers throughout the country and beyond have been experimenting with ways of making learning intentions and success criteria more accessible to children. Cats, dogs, dragons and wise owls have provided appeal. Acronyms such as WALT (*We are learning to...*) and WILF

(*What I'm looking for…*) have been used to capture children's interest. The feedback I have received from countless children, teachers and schools is that sharing learning intentions and developing success criteria leads to visible changes in the classroom: children and teachers are more focused on the learning than the activity, and children are more hardworking, cooperative, self-evaluative and confident.

However, the results of the children's interviews in the Gillingham Project showed that the various devices can muddle children about the real purpose of these things. Children were asked to say what the board at the front of the class was about and what it was for. We wanted them to say something as simple as (for the learning intention) *'That's what we're learning'* and (for the success criteria) *'That's what we have to do to learn it'*. Where characters had been attributed rather too much power, for example, children said they were learning *for the character*. Even when prompted (*'Does anyone else want you to learn – like the teacher or you?'*), they still insisted that the character was the main interested party! Where teachers used the acronym WILF for the success criteria, children explained that those were the things *the teacher* wanted you to do. Of course this was their response, and we should not have been surprised: the words 'What *I'm* looking for' were repeated lesson after lesson.

Children clearly took on board the rationale implicitly given to them by the characters or the acronyms. This is not to say that the impact of sharing learning intentions and using success criteria had not been fruitful – it certainly was – but if we care about how children are perceiving their role as learners, we need to take notice of these findings. Perhaps we, the adults, more than the children, needed a way of making something abstract more concrete and accessible.

I now recommend that we use the simplest possible language and provide a clear rationale for children for the purpose of any formative assessment strategy, whether it is derived from my books, other teacher's ideas or people's own ideas. It seems that, unless teachers say otherwise, children automatically assume that any new process in the classroom is a tool for the benefit of the teacher rather than the child. When we asked children the purpose of the list of self-evaluation questions used as a prompt by the teacher, for instance, they mainly said it was *'for the teacher to find out what we can do and what we can't do'*. This was far from the purpose. The questions were used to get children to reflect on their learning and analyse their learning needs. Formative assessment is, in many ways, about making very explicit to children things that teachers have done for years but held as their own.

With a plea that teachers should beware of children not being able to 'see the wood for the trees', here are two very simple ways of labeling learning intentions and success criteria so that the purpose stays clear. Notice that the first is a 'bits' learning intention – the skill of letter writing. The second is an 'application' learning intention, although in earlier years children will have encountered it as a writing skill in the 'bits' category.

We are learning to …	… write a letter.
Remember to …	■ Write your address and date at the top on the right
	■ Start with *Dear*.
	■ Write to the three bears saying sorry.
	■ Say why you did it.
	■ Finish by writing *Love from*.

OR

Learning intention	Write an effective characterisation.
	What will you need to do to achieve this?
Success criteria	Include some or all of the following:
	■ hobbies and interests,
	■ personality type,
	■ attitude to self/others,
	■ sense of humour,
	■ examples of your friend's character.

Knowing the overall rationale for the learning intention

Children need to know *why* they are covering the learning intention at all. Teachers in the Gillingham Project were asked somehow to include this information in a lesson. Overall, teachers either *told* children the rationale for the learning intention or *asked them* for their ideas. Time management seems important here, but a few moments spent *asking* children for their ideas was thought to be more helpful in focusing, motivating and helping the learning process to be more effective.

Teachers felt that having a ritualistic approach for the 'big picture' (i.e. every lesson and always at the same time) was inappropriate, because some lessons, especially literacy lessons, would result in repetition. Discussing the rationale for the learning intention is sometimes appropriate as part of the teaching section (e.g. *'When might you need to know about fractions?'*), sometimes at the beginning of the lesson, and sometimes not at all, if it is part of an ongoing theme. Overall, teachers felt that this was an important element, but should be left to the teacher's discretion.

Some examples of ways in which teachers either 'told' or 'asked' children about the reason for the learning

Teachers **telling** children

Some teachers linked the rationale for the learning intention to the *school world* and others to the *wider world*. Links to the **school world** tended to be focused on how the learning would be helpful in their future work:

Y1 teacher: *'This is because this will help you to spell words correctly in your writing.'*

Y2 teacher: *'It will help us to use dictionaries and word books more easily.'*

Y4 teacher: *'If you understand how cinquains and acrostics work you will have a wider choice of writing types to choose from (and have more fun).'*

Links to the **wider world** were
... sometimes *analytical*:
In a Y5 lesson, children were asked to think about ships 500 years ago, listen to information given and work in pairs to work out the important crew members. The teacher said that *'decision-making with logical reasoning is an important "life skill"'*.

... sometimes *social*:
In a Y6 symmetry lesson, the teacher explained *'We are learning to recognise and find a <u>half</u> of different shapes'* and her rationale was *'so we are able to share things equally, like when I broke the biscuit in half, it was not exactly half, so one person would get more than the other.'*

... sometimes *practical*:
In a Y6 classroom children were learning to find the area of straight-sided irregular shapes. The teacher's rationale was *'The reason we are doing this is because in the real world there are lots of things which are irregular shapes such as my garden and my living room and sometimes we need to work out their areas.'*

Teachers *asking* children

Some teachers asked children for their ideas about the rationale for the learning intention. Children's comments which linked to the **school world**, tended to be focused on how the learning would be helpful in their future work, lead to personal improvement or prepare them for the next stage:

Y4 teacher: *'Why are we doing this?'* (English comprehension)
Child: **'So you can do it better than you did in September.'**

Y6 teacher: *'Why do you think we're doing this?'*
Child: **'For our secondary school.'**

Links made by children to the **wider world** were
... sometimes *analytical*:
Y6 teacher: 'Think generally, why are we doing this?'(design technology: making a mock-up before making a final version)
Child: **'Thinking things through before you do them is a good idea!'**

... sometimes *social*:
Y6 teacher: 'Why have we done this today?' (children had been learning about stereotyping)
Child: **'So you don't do it to everyone else.'**
Child: **'So you don't judge people and hurt them.'**

Y5 teacher: 'Why do you need to know "time"?'
Child: **'To stop us being late.'**

Y4 teacher: 'We have been learning about Sikh symbols. Why is it important to learn about the bigger picture?'
Child: **'So everybody's included.'**
Teacher: 'Yes. So that we know there's a range of ways of doing things and not just our own ways.'

... sometimes *practical*:
Y1 teacher: 'Why do you think we need to learn this?' (counting)
Child: **'When we're older we need to count.'**
Teacher: 'Why?'
Child: **'We need to know about money.'**
Child: **'We need to go shopping.'**

Y4 teacher: 'Why do we need to know alphabetical order? Where would we use it?'
Child: **'We need it if we need to find something in the Library.'**
Child: **'We see alphabetical order in the Phone book.'**

Key principles

- Delivery and coverage with poor understanding are pointless and even harmful.

- There are two main types of learning intentions: knowledge, concepts and skills (taught specifics) and applications (the applying of the first within the 'whole context').

■ Alternating the two types of learning intentions furthers the learning.

■ Learning intentions need to be explicitly separated from the context of the activity, except for knowledge, where the context is part of the learning intention.

■ Children need to know how all the learning intentions for a unit of study fit together.

■ Share learning intentions and success criteria in simple ways, so that children see that the purpose is to enhance their learning.

■ It is useful for children to know the real-life rationale for their learning.

INSET ideas

1. In a staff meeting, brainstorm ideas for reducing coverage. Then circulate the ideas on pages 18–19 and get teachers to try any of the combined ideas over a few weeks. Feed back and discuss the impact of these strategies. Agree a whole-school approach for where the priorities must lie and the minimum expectation.
2. Bring the last few weeks' short-term plans to a staff meeting and introduce the 'bits' and 'application' learning intentions. Get teachers, in pairs or groups, to analyse their lessons and feed back on their findings. They could then together plan any adjustments and feed back.
3. Using their short-term plans, teachers in pairs separate learning intentions from context. Feed back findings and discuss.
4. Brainstorm current practice and ideas for giving children a way of seeing all the learning intentions to be covered for a particular area of study. Ask teachers to try out their own ideas or the suggestion on page 25. Feed back a few weeks later.
5. Share the findings from interviews with children about the use of characters and acronyms (e.g. Walt and Wilf) and discuss. Decide on any modifications.

3 Success criteria

(Assessment Reform Group, 2002)

Definitive success criteria

For some time, many teachers mainly focused success criteria around end-points and products, using words like *'By the end you will have…'*. The Gillingham study revealed that 'product' success criteria were relatively unhelpful for children compared to 'process' success criteria.

Examples of 'product' success criteria which are **less helpful** for children

Example 1
Learning intention: *To be able to use papier mâché effectively.*
Success criterion: Everyone will have made a bowl.

Example 2
Learning intention: *To be able to identify odd and even numbers.*
Success criterion: Your answers will be correct.

Example 3
Learning intention: *To write an effective characterisation.*
Success criterion: Someone who reads it will feel they really know the person.

These success criteria are broadly what the teacher wants, but they do not indicate, for the children, how the learning intention is to be fulfilled. There is a definite feeling of *'I'll know it when I see it'*, which leaves both the teacher and the learner in reactive rather than proactive mode.

Instinctively, a number of Gillingham teachers created success criteria with children which were focused around the **process**, or *how* the learning intention would be achieved. In these classrooms, children were actively engaged in the process of learning, using the success criteria as an aide-memoire of the necessary ingredients.

The same learning intentions with 'process' success criteria

Example 1 ('Bit' learning intention)
Learning intention: *To be able to use papier mâché effectively.*
Success criteria: Remember to:

■ tear up the paper;

■ cover it with the paste;

■ smooth it around the balloon evenly.

Example 2 ('Bit' learning intention')
Learning intention: *To be able to identify odd and even numbers.*
Success criteria: Use one or both of:

■ look at the last digit in the number to check the pattern;

■ divide the number by two to check.

Example 3 ('Application' learning intention)
Learning intention: *To write an effective characterisation.*
Success criteria: Include all or some, with examples:

■ whether they are extrovert/introvert;

■ hobbies and interests;

■ attitude to themselves/to others;

■ what makes that person your friend.

Success criteria need to be brief and succinct, a summary of what has been discussed so far, so they may make reference to more elaborate descriptions on the whiteboard or around the room, as in the success criteria given for Example 2. The children, for this lesson, have the odd and even sequence pattern already displayed, so the success criterion can simply refer to this. Written on the whiteboard are also examples of numbers divided by two, demonstrating how this shows whether they are even or odd, so this is again a 'shorthand' version.

Once success criteria are visible in the room (90 per cent of what the brain remembers is derived from visual images!), children often look up while they are working to check that they are on task. Whenever I work with adults now, I only give tasks if they are accompanied by a learning intention and success criteria – adult learners need the same visual prompts. You can believe you understand a task presented to you at the time, but, once you are engaged in the actual activity, it is easy to lose track of the whole point of the exercise. The visual success criteria keep everyone focused.

The skills, concepts and knowledge learning intentions ('bits') have success criteria which are usually chronological and step by step. Following them usually ensures success and often ensures quality.

The 'application' learning intentions, on the other hand, usually have success criteria which were once 'bits' and tend to be a list of ingredients in no particular order. Using them ensures that the learning intention has been met, although quality is not ensured.

Quality

The issue of quality is important when discussing success criteria. The purpose of children having success criteria is not to give them a simple fix-it list, but rather to remind them of those aspects of the task on which they most need to focus. Quality can only be ensured by the teacher's modelling, her questioning, the level of discussion in the classroom and the quality of the different forms of feedback given. In writing an effective characterisation, for example, it will be the examples given and modelling of such writing, the quality of the process during the lesson, and the quality of the feedback offered to the child by other children or adults, that will finally ensure the overall quality of the child's work.

The QCA Assessment for Learning website (www.qca.org.uk) stresses the importance of modelling quality through a variety of means:

■ *encouraging pupils to listen to the range of pupils' responses to questions;*

> ■ *showing pupils the learning strategies;*
>
> ■ *showing pupils how the assessment criteria have been met in some examples of work from children not known to the pupils;*
>
> ■ *encouraging pupils to review examples from anonymous pupils that do not meet the assessment criteria, in order to suggest the next steps to meeting the assessment criteria;*
>
> ■ *using examples of work from other pupils in the class highlighting the ways it meets the assessment criteria or standards.* **9**

Better planning in less time!

Once the success criteria have been planned and written in the short-term plan, something magical follows – the activity agenda is now set, so less time needs to be spent on the planning of the activity. This, in turn, means that when it comes to asking children for the success criteria, there is no mystery. The lesson has been structured around these very things, so gathering success criteria amounts to no more than *getting children to summarise the teaching points made so far.*

To encourage children to take responsibility for their learning, it is important to ask children for the success criteria, just before they go about the task. This should simply be a process of giving back, in summary form, the main teaching points made which link directly to the learning intention. Knowing what is required to meet the learning intention places the learner in a powerful position of control. The **learner** can now:

■ keep track of what has been done and what still needs to be done in the time available;

■ know the expectation of the teacher;

■ start to self-evaluate against the criteria, seeking help where needed (*'This bit was fine..., this bit I'm not quite sure about...'*);

■ be in a position to mark his or her own work or cooperate with a response partner;

■ confidently work with others who share the same criteria.

The LEARN Project (University of Bristol, 2000) found that children were often unclear about the requirements of tasks and had little understanding of quality.

Teachers find the benefits of having success criteria far-reaching:

■ Planning is focused more around success criteria than the activity, which saves time and clarifies the lesson.

■ Planning for success criteria can involve discovering that the activity will not meet the learning intention in its present form, necessitating activity modification.

■ Oral feedback during the course of a lesson focuses naturally around the success criteria.

■ Marking is more focused around success criteria than superficial, limited features.

■ The need for individual targets decreases as teachers' and children's concerns become more focused around meeting success criteria.

Change the planning space!

We have been locked into an activity culture ever since the onset of the National Curriculum, and I believe this stems not only from overloaded coverage, but also from the design of lesson planning sheets. The widest column in a plan will clearly dominate planning time and thinking time. It follows therefore that the lesson is likely to be activity-led if more time was spent planning this than any other feature of the lesson. The danger is, of course, that thoroughly planned lessons lead teachers to feel that they should endeavour to get through everything, regardless of whether it fulfils the learning intention as the lesson progresses. The needs of the learning intention (*are the children learning what we have set out to learn?*) should be our prime concern during the course of a lesson or series of lessons, with adjustments made as a matter of course.

Imagine if the widest column in the planning sheet was entitled '*Effective questions*' or '*Ways of raising children's self-esteem during this lesson*'. The 'message' would be clear: this is what teachers need to spend more planning time on. Thus pedagogy itself is determined by the amount of space allocated on a planning sheet. No planning sheets have ever been statutory in the UK – they are provided as *suggested* formats, mainly because teachers would complain if they were all left to their own devices. The Qualifications and Curriculum Authority (QCA) schemes of work stemmed from requests from teachers. However, once 'suggested' documents become printed, they take on an air of officialdom.

An example of headings in a plan in which the success criteria lead

Literacy

Learning intention	Context	Success criteria (*what you need to do to achieve the learning intention*)	Organisation (*activity, resources, differentiation in brief*)	Notes for future planning (*if nec*)

This is simply an example of how schools are free to develop their own plans with their own rationale, to make the teaching and the learning work *for* them rather than against them. Schools using this model and other similar models (where the success criteria come before the activity) have tried it successfully with Literacy and Numeracy, now believing that they have those subjects embedded well enough not to have to write every detail of a lesson on a plan. Under 'Organisation' they divide the lesson up into its various parts.

Linking what has been said so far about planning and learning intentions and success criteria, the following examples come from INSET sessions I have run in the last year. Teachers were asked to take a recent lesson and write it into the first columns of the planning sheet. After feedback and discussion, these examples were produced. More examples are included in the photocopiable resources available on the Hodder website (see page viii).

Examples of learning intentions separated from the context and success criteria

Literacy

Subject	Learning intention	Context	Success criteria (*what you need to do to achieve the learning intention*) *These are planned, determine the teaching of the lesson and are gathered from the children and written up just before they start to work*
Literacy Y5	To write complex sentences.	*The Jungle Book*	■ Use appropriate connectives. ■ Include main and subordinate clauses. ■ Vary the position of the sub-clause for effect.
Literacy Y2	To be able to write instructions.	Making jelly	■ Write everything in the correct order. ■ Use bullet points, numbers or first, second, etc. ■ Use imperatives (bossy verbs). ■ Use your scaffold sheet.

Numeracy

Numeracy Reception	To be able to count in two sets using practical apparatus.	Farm animals	Remember to: ■ count the animals in the first group; ■ carry on the counting with the second group; ■ move each animal as you count it.

Science

Subject	Learning intention	Context	Success criteria (*what you need to do to achieve the learning intention*) *These are planned, determine the teaching of the lesson and are gathered from the children and written up just before they start to work*
Science Y3	To know the meaning of the terms *translucent*, *transparent* and *opaque*.	Shining light through materials.	Remember to: ■ use the light source; ■ decide which group the material belongs to and put it in the right group; ■ use the definitions on the whiteboard if you are unsure.

ICT

ICT Y3	To be able to use word processing skills.	Writing about ourselves.	Remember to use some or all of: ■ font, size and colour; ■ pictures; ■ positioning; ■ effects (bullet points, etc).
ICT Y2	To program repeat and pendown functions.	Rotating patterns using the Roamer.	Remember to: ■ program the shape; ■ put the pen down; ■ use the Repeat function to rotate the shape.

Foundation Subjects

Geography Y5	To understand the positive and negative effects of human activity on the environment.	Tourism (research effects on St Lucia)	Remember to: ■ classify the effects into positive and negative; ■ discuss the negative effects and think of a solution.
Music Y1	To be able to perform a piece of music as a group.	Stone age rain dance	Remember: ■ work cooperatively; ■ structure; ■ rehearse; ■ rhythm and pulse.
RE Y4	To understand the importance of religious artifacts in worship.	Judaism in the home	Remember to: ■ name the artifacts; ■ discuss their use; ■ explain why they are important.

Success criteria often highlight a mis-match between learning intention and task

Some schools have redesigned their short-term planning sheets in this way to make the success criteria the widest column and making the activity more succinct. Their findings have been welcome — planning takes less time and lessons are more focused around learning intentions and success criteria. Teachers also find that planning success criteria leads to sometimes rethinking the activity to meet the learning intention more appropriately.

While recently working with a group of teachers, the following example of this arose:

Learning intention: *To know the most significant features of the Sikh religion.*
Planned activity: *Teacher input, children given resource material, then asked to write three paragraphs summarising the three significant features.*

While developing the success criteria, the teachers realised that the lesson would not work – many children would not get past the first paragraph and children would be focusing more on spellings and their writing than the learning in hand. The Gillingham Project revealed that a mis-match between learning intention and task most often involved children in doing too much recording rather than discussion about the learning. Teachers feel under pressure to have children's recording everywhere. What matters is the *amount* of recording and whether it is appropriate for the learning intention of the lesson. The lesson was changed as follows:

Planned activity: *Teacher input, children given resource material and asked to present from each table one of the significant features to the rest of the class. The teacher and class together devised three sentences to summarise their findings and then wrote them in their books* (abbreviated on the plan).

An indicator of the success of a lesson/s is whether the children can tell you what they have been learning. When the learning intention is adhered to in the design of the activity, reflected in the success criteria, this is a much more likely occurrence.

Anecdotes from INSET: the importance of analysing and discussing as a staff

During INSET, I ask teachers to take a recent lesson and try to separate the learning intention from the context and then decide the success criteria for the lesson. These are then read out and all participants contribute in order to arrive at the most suitable words, as the previous example shows. Sometimes the learning intention or the success criteria need to be reworded. The following anecdotes might be useful in showing the significance of these discussions, and how important it is for staff to go through this process together before being asked to plan in this way *on their own*. The learning curve is steep – the first time this is done takes the longest.

Knowledge context stays in the learning intention!

Anecdote 1

It is important to remember that the knowledge learning intentions have to include the context. For example, one group said that their learning intention was *'To know significant events in history'* and that the context was *'The Gunpowder Plot'*. If this learning intention is shared with children, the success criteria will be impossible to generate and feedback will be unfocused. As it is *knowledge*, the learning intention should read *'To know the key events of the Gunpowder Plot'* and the context would be, say, *'Drama and writing'*.

Sorting out the learning intention

Anecdote 2

A learning intention from one RE scheme had the learning intention *'To know what the local vicar does'* (!). Problems were caused because this learning intention was actually the context. The teachers decided that what they wanted the children to learn was not what the vicar does, but *'To know the duties of religious leaders'* – with the context of finding out what the local vicar does. With this refocus, the success criteria and the whole lesson becomes clearer.

Anecdote 3

Another group produced the IT learning intention *'To program instructions in the Roamer'*. Through subsequent questioning, they agreed that they wanted the children to learn to program instructions in a specific way, and not necessarily using a Roamer. The learning intention was changed to *'To program repeat and pendown functions'* and the context was *'Repeating patterns using the Roamer'*.

Changing the activity

Anecdote 4

Mathematics lessons may well have differentiated activities. One example of a learning intention was *'To be able to sequence numbers'*. The context given was *'ordering to 10 with number cards'*. The discussion revolved around the need for differentiation, leading to a change of context. It was decided that the class would have different sets of numbered cards (0–10, 0–100, etc), so the context would now read 'Numbered cards'. Instead of success criteria focused on numbers to 10, they were able to be focused on the ordering process and suitable for all levels of ability:

Success criteria: Remember to:

■ start with the smallest number;

■ look at the value of the numbers;

■ finish with the largest number.

How many success criteria?

Anecdote 5

Learning intention: To be able to measure accurately to the nearest cm, and record.
Context: Measuring classroom objects.
Activity: Input rounding to the nearest cm. Children to measure width of classroom objects from given list with cm tape, and record.

Success criteria: Remember to:

■ start from zero;

■ use the rounding rules;

■ record the unit.

In this example, there are three parts to the learning intention: *to measure accurately, the nearest cm* and *record*. The purpose of success criteria is to give children an accessible aide-memoire, so it is important not to end up with a list of dozens of criteria, especially for younger children. Where the learning intention consists of multiple elements, it is probably better to choose just one significant success criterion for each, as in this example of measuring. We don't need to remind them of everything they have ever known about measuring, just what they are most likely to forget at this stage.

Differentiation

Teachers often worry about differentiation and success criteria, imagining that there might be, say, four lists of success criteria because children are involved in different tasks. As long as teachers stick to the principle that all children should have access to the same learning intention if they are roughly the same age, and the role of the teacher is to give them *access* to it, the success criteria will be the same for all children. For example, given the learning intention *'To use effective adjectives'*, the worst thing we could do would be to marginalise a group of children who cannot yet write their name. They must, of course, be given an activity in which they find effective adjectives, but orally. So there might be pairs using their senses to find words to describe a flower they are looking at, other groups devising adjectives to put before given nouns with pictures, and some children writing free sentences in which they use effective adjectives. Regardless of their task, the children will all need the same success criteria:

■ Use all your senses in choosing the words.

■ Put the adjective before the noun.

■ It should make the described object easier to imagine.

Mathematics lessons are rather different. Children still need access to the same learning intention, but because of the specific nature of mathematics skills, access is often achieved by giving children easier versions of the same skill, which require different rules. While learning about long multiplication, some children might be using a non-standard algorithm while others might be working on simple repeated addition. Here some compromise might have to take place – all success criteria written up would be too time-consuming, so teachers in this situation tend to tell children the success criteria as they set the groups off. If the criteria are not too lengthy, it is possible to write them on a piece of paper which is then placed in the middle of each table, or, if a classroom assistant is present, she can be asked to write the success criteria as soon as the group has been set off.

Children's views about learning intentions and success criteria

Teachers and children were interviewed in the Gillingham Project about the impact of learning intentions and success criteria. Almost all children said that they liked to know this information. The reasons they gave were:

(i) Knowing the success criteria led to children trying to meet the success criteria.
'Because you want to know – to learn things.'

(ii) Knowing the criteria guided their thoughts before they started a task.
'Because it makes me think before working.'

(iii) Knowing the success criteria sharpened children's focus.
'The success criteria give you pinpoints you have to work towards. You might be worried about handwriting, but that may not be the success criteria – if the success criteria says punctuation and paragraphs, then you concentrate on punctuation and paragraphs.'

(iv) Having the success criteria visible meant children could refer to them as they worked.
'It's more useful, easier if it's written on the board 'cause sometimes I forget.'

Teachers' views about learning intentions and success criteria

The majority of teachers believed that children liked having learning intentions and success criteria. They said that children:

■ **were more focused on the task**
'It stops them from straying off task and keeps them focused on the learning intention.' (Y4 teacher)

■ **have clearer expectations**
'I really think it's important that learning is meaningful, that children know why they are doing work and what you expect from them. I was never given this information as a child. I think it raises expectations for the children and the teachers.' (Y5 teacher)

■ **show more concentration**
'It takes the load off them. They can join in. They can concentrate on the work ahead.' (Y4 teacher)

■ **show that they want to know what they are learning**
'They're the same as us. They take more interest in something if they know what, why and how.' (Y4 teacher)

■ **take more ownership of their learning**
'They go home and say what they've learnt in a clear and sophisticated way. The parents like to hear what they say and they feel they've done some learning today instead of the usual talk about dinners.' (Y6 teacher)

■ **check their own and each other's work against success criteria**
'They like the power of it. They know what they're doing and can check their own and each other's work to make sure they are getting it right.' (Y1 teacher)

■ **work more quickly**
'They are more able to work quicker to meet the goal.' (Y1 teacher)

■ **were more motivated and settled**
'They like knowing the goal. They are now more motivated and less afraid to make mistakes.' (Y2 teacher)

■ **were more articulate, with increased vocabulary**
'Their vocabulary has developed as a result of this. It focuses their learning.' (Reception teacher)

■ **refer to the learning intention and success criteria**
'They go back to it, they are more focused because they know exactly what I'm looking for. They're much clearer about what needs to be done in the lesson.' (Y2 teacher)

■ **were no longer asking the teacher for task instructions**
'They are free now to work out and have a go at what they have to do.' (Y5 teacher)

■ **were more independent**
'It creates a degree of independence. They know what they are doing and they go away and get on.' (Y4 teacher)

Most teachers said that knowing the success criteria was the key ingredient in aiding understanding and that older children clearly used the success criteria to check their achievement.

Teacher's comments included:

'One of the lower ability children has changed from a boy who always felt he didn't know anything to having a very positive attitude and now attempts to try things.' (Y2 teacher)

'They have a much deeper understanding. They really can pick up on the learning intention and apply it in the next lesson and remember it.' (Y1 teacher)

'The task is clearer as it's more defined. The children are also involved in more discussion, which aids understanding.' (Y6 teacher)

'I can see the benefits of knowing the success criteria. Their answers show they have used it as a guide to what they chose to put down and it's no longer just neatness that they concentrate on. They told me they hold the success criteria in their minds as they work. I see a big difference. In marked work there are fewer mistakes in their knowledge of facts.' (Y6 teacher)

Key principles

■ Process success criteria are more powerful than product success criteria.

■ Success criteria need to be planned in advance.

■ Planning success criteria leads to more focused activities and less overplanning of activities.

■ The widest column in a planning sheet tends to dictate the teaching and planning focus.

■ Schools can decide how to make their planning effective.

■ Success criteria should be generic for all children, regardless of their task, as long as they all have access to the same learning intention (exception: some mathematics).

■ Success criteria need to be gathered from the children to give them ownership.

■ Quality comes from the teaching and feedback, not the success criteria.

INSET ideas

1. Introduce the findings about process success criteria and give examples. Get teachers to review their current practice through discussion. Go through some of the examples available via the website (see page viii) one at a time with the whole staff, giving them all the information except the success criteria. In pairs, they decide on the success criteria. Decide together on the best success criteria, then compare to the success criteria given in the examples. If there is a discrepancy, discuss together why that might be. All this takes time, but it's worth it!

2. Next get teachers to bring along their short-term plans and, in pairs, take one activity and write it into the first four columns of the photocopiable planning sheet which is also available on the website (Subject, Learning Intention, Context and Success Criteria). Get the pairs to read them out. Discuss them as a whole staff, tweaking the words till they are acceptable (this might involve changing any part of the plan). Go round all pairs. If this is a half-day session, get teachers to do another activity straight away, building on what they have learnt through these discussions. It should be quicker! Feed back findings again. Do it again with a third activity (make sure they are different subject areas each time).

3. After this INSET ask teachers to try planning one subject in this way to begin with, gradually introducing the other subjects. Feed back in two weeks to discuss findings and ways forward.

What matters about feedback

'The most powerful single moderator that enhances achievement is feedback.'

(Hattie, 1992)

'Teachers should be aware of the impact that comments, marks and grades can have on learners' confidence and enthusiasm and should be as constructive as possible in the feedback that they give.'

(Assessment Reform Group, 2002)

Whether feedback is oral or written, there are some key features which can be drawn from a great deal of classroom research.

The comparison effect

When the Black and Wiliam (1998) review of formative assessment was published, the aspect which received most media attention was their findings about teachers' feedback to children. The traditional forms of feedback have, in many cases, led to regression in children's progress. One of the key negative elements is the giving of grades for every piece of work, but there are many more subtle things, such as the teacher's tone of voice, body language, how difficulty with learning is talked about, the use of teaching assistants with certain children, and the words used by teachers when interacting with children.

Hargreaves, McCallum and Gipps (2001), in their research of feedback strategies used by teachers, found a range of 'approval' and 'disapproval' strategies. Non-verbal strategies for expressing approval included the teacher nodding, making eye contact, smiling, laughing, putting an arm around or patting the child and taking on a mild manner in order to be approachable. Non-verbal means of expressing disapproval included pulling faces, staring hard, clicking fingers or making disapproving noises. All of these strategies give clear messages to children about how the teacher feels about their ability.

Comparisons with other children are made all the time in our classrooms – in the ways described above – so that children are continually aware of how their abilities compare to others. This has a direct impact on their self-efficacy, or how they perceive their abilities. By giving children feedback about how they have done *against the criteria of the task*, children are released from these comparisons and given breathing space to move forward.

Many secondary schools are now trialling 'comment only' marking, with grades awarded only at end of units, with increased achievement as a result.

External rewards, such as merit marks and stickers, act in the same way as grades, demoralising the less able and making complacent the more able. They signify approval, but do not help children know how to 'close the gap' between present performance and future goals. Children who have put effort into their work can feel that this was pointless if they do not receive a reward.

Key findings about the use of external rewards indicate that:

- Students strive for the reward, not the achievement.

- They encourage competition, rather than cooperation.

- They conflict with deep thinking and investigation (one finds the quickest route to get the reward).

- They make complacent the more able and demoralise the less able.

- Average students get them the least.

- They have short-term motivational gains (effective when classroom circumstances are dire, such as very poor pupil behaviour).

Ways forward

Terry Crooks (2001), as a result of his review of literature about feedback and the link with pupil motivation, concluded that:

‘ *the greatest motivational benefits will come from focusing feedback on:*

■ *the qualities of the child's work, and not on comparison with other children;*

■ *specific ways in which the child's work could be improved;*

■ *improvements that the child has made compared to his or her earlier work.* ’

Specific and *improved* are two key words in Crook's recommendations. We have tended to be too general in the past to be helpful to children (e.g. *'some good words here'* or broad targets such as *'remember to use more exciting adjectives'*). We have also tended to focus feedback on correction rather than improvement. On the whole, feedback has been a mainly negative experience for most children. Token comments at the bottom of work praising effort do not fool children, because the grades or rewards, and spelling and grammar corrections, tell children the 'truth' about their work.

The 'LEARN' Project (University of Bristol, 2000 – see www.qca.org.uk) consisted of interviews with over 200 pupils between Years 3 and 13 about their perceptions of assessment. The key findings were:

■ Pupils were often confused by effort and attainment grades.

■ Pupils sometimes felt that their effort was not recognised by teachers.

■ Pupils preferred feedback that was prompt and delivered orally.

■ Pupils were often unable to use feedback effectively.

■ Pupils felt that feedback that was constructively critical helped improve their performance.

My own research has added to this:

- Children believe that the purpose of marking is for the teacher to find out what they have got right or wrong, rather than for their own benefit.

- Children are rarely given time to read marking comments.

- Children often cannot understand or read the teachers' handwriting or comments.

- Children are rarely given time to make any improvement on their work because of the teacher's feeling of pressure to get on with coverage.

The Gillingham Project (2000–1) focused mainly on giving oral or written feedback that told children where they had achieved success and where they could improve (for individual pieces of work). These findings are illustrated in the next chapter, along with examples of children's work.

The Assessment Reform Group (2002), in *Assessment for Learning: Ten Principles*, said, as a result of collating the research about feedback:

‘ *Assessment that encourages learning fosters motivation by emphasising progress and achievement rather than failure. Comparison with others who have been more successful is unlikely to motivate learners. It can also lead to their withdrawing from the learning process in areas where they have been made to feel they are 'no good'. Motivation can be preserved and enhanced by assessment methods which protect the learner's autonomy, provide some choice and constructive feedback, and create opportunity for self-direction.*

Learners need information and guidance in order to plan next steps in their learning. Teachers should: pinpoint the learner's strengths and advise on how to develop them; be clear and constructive about any weaknesses and how they might be addressed; provide opportunities for learners to improve upon their work. ’

Key principles

■ Feedback needs to be focused on the learning intention of the task and not on comparisons with other children.

■ Verbal and non-verbal language from the teacher gives powerful messages to the child about his or her ability.

■ Grading every piece of work leads to demoralisation for lower achievers and complacency for higher achievers.

■ External rewards act like grades.

■ We need to give *specific* feedback focusing on success and improvement, rather than correction.

■ Children need opportunities to make improvements on their work.

INSET ideas

1. Get paired teachers to observe each other teaching any lesson for 30 minutes, taking notes under the following headings:

   ■ Body language which boosts/lowers self-esteem;

   ■ Verbal language which boosts/lowers self-esteem;

   ■ Tone of voice which boosts/lowers self-esteem.

   Pairs compare notes after both have been observed and present findings at a staff meeting. Implications of the findings need to lead to action.

2. As a staff, trial comment-only marking (grading at end of units) if grades are normally given for every piece of work.

5 The teacher's language – enabling a feedback culture

'Pupils need to have the skills to ask for help and the ethos of the school should encourage them to do so.'
(QCA website: www.qca.org.uk – Assessment for Learning link)

Oral feedback is the most natural and frequent feedback experience for children: feedback from the teacher, to the teacher and from and to peers. At its best, it is tailor-made and powerful in meeting the needs of the child. At worst, it confirms low self-efficacy and silences children into 'victim' mode.

Celebrating challenge

The language of the classroom, especially the incidental talk that goes on while children are working, gives strong messages to children about their ability. For example:

'I know you are having difficulty with this. Don't worry – I'm going to help you.'

Here, the child is likely to have two feelings at once: she is grateful that she will receive help, but the fact that she needs help has reinforced for her that she is somehow lacking compared to her peers. If this had been said to all the children, the child's self-esteem would not be affected. It is the 'comparison' effect that causes problems.

The answer seems to lie in shifting our thinking about the way in which children should tackle or face difficulties. It is generally accepted that without an element of 'the creased brow effect' or some 'thinking', learning is probably not taking place. We are simply going over things we already know (a situation many children experience in classrooms). If this is the case, then perhaps we should be indicating the importance and necessity of this when talking to children.

Children tend to see themselves as mainly attempting to please the teacher and to be seen to be finding everything easy. How often have you heard children say to each other, or themselves *'This is easy!'*, as if the whole point of school is to do things you already know how to do! This fear of failure is deeply embedded and can only be tackled by, at the least, a complete change in the way in which we talk to children in the classroom.

Teachers in the Gillingham Project were asked to change the way in which they talked to children about encountering a level of challenge in their work as key to the learning process:

'It's OK, that's how you learn'.
'It's OK if you find it hard. It shows you are really trying to work it out.'
'It's making you think because you are learning something you didn't know before and I am here to help.'
'I'm glad you asked about that when you found it hard. It means that others will be able to learn from my explanation to you.'
'When you find something challenging, it is an opportunity to learn something new.'
'Now you'll learn something that you didn't know before. Then it won't be hard the next time you meet it.'
'This is how we learn. If everything is easy, it means you had already known how to do it, so there's no new learning.'

Or, as one Y6 teacher put it:
'So it didn't make anybody really think? So it was a waste of time – you knew it all!'

These teachers said that they had noticed, as a result of this language, that children were less afraid to make mistakes, that children with special education needs and those of higher ability had increased their self-esteem and that children were more able now to admit their difficulties. Some quotes from teachers illustrate these findings:

    ❝ *The impact is their increased confidence and willingness to own up that something is wrong. It has stopped them wanting to be first to finish. They are more inclined to do more work and are getting more motivated.* ❞

(Y2 teacher)

> ❝ *I use the language a lot. I have a high percentage of children in the class who are SEN and they hear me say that to bright kids and I say it when I find things difficult. I think it boosts the SEN children's self-esteem to know that everyone finds some things difficult.* ❞
>
> (Y6 teacher)

> ❝ *I use it all the time. It has brought the top ones in who were cocky and couldn't admit that something was difficult. They're now all saying when something's hard. Some are saying I don't want your help, so it's making them more independent. They're choosing to work on it themselves. They're now repeating the words of it being important to find it difficult.* ❞
>
> (Y2 teacher)

Using this language in the classroom creates an ethos where speaking freely about learning is OK. This not only enables children to be more willing to articulate their self-evaluation, but also to more readily give feedback to teachers and each other.

Of course, following this course of action leads to some inevitable consequences. Children more confidently ask for help and say that they are doing work which is not making them think enough. When asked for help, teachers need to have strategies. The following poster gives a step-by-step approach to self-help when things are challenging.

Self-help: how to help yourself when something really makes you think

1. Don't worry or panic.
2. Remind yourself that if it makes you think, you are learning something new.
3. Read it again — think it through.
4. Ask a friend, see how they have got on so far.
5. Use class resources — number squares, dictionaries, etc.
6. Ask an adult.

More confidence to self-evaluate

Gillingham teachers were asked to introduce self-evaluation discussions with children, using questions such as *'What were you pleased with about (the learning intention)?'* or *'What really made you think about (the learning intention)?'* As a result of the change of language when children encountered difficulty, they were much more confident about articulating areas of need.

Many children were pleased when the teacher asked about difficulty, because they knew if they spoke up, the teacher would help them, or get others to suggest strategies:

'I like to answer why I didn't get it. The teacher or someone will clear things up.' (Average Y5)

'"What did you find difficult?" helps most because then he explains it in a better way and you understand it more.' (Above-average Y6)

'The best one for me is when I say what was hard. I get lots of help and the next time I do it good.' (Below-average Y3)

Some able juniors learnt from listening to others explaining why they found something easy or difficult:

'I like to listen when people say why they found something easy. Because you can save it in your head to help you later.' (Above-average Y5)

During our observations, it was possible to see a range of teachers' reactions when children explained what they had found difficult about trying to achieve success. Beyond the strategies of delving and getting children to explain to bring their strategies to light, other strategies that were more 'formative' and more likely to create a learning climate were:

■ to tell children they were not the only ones to have those difficulties and that they would be getting more practice so not to worry;

■ to give positive feedback to a child or children (publicly) about the parts they had done well (and explaining how this was 'well on the way' to achieving success or how this related well to the learning intention);

■ to go over to the child (privately) and suggest strategies for 'next time' or invite the child to try again.

Less useful reactions were:

- to show disbelief they were really having difficulties and praise children for something they had done (not always related to the learning intention or the success criteria);

- to ignore a child's comment and move on to the next child with a hand up;

- to commiserate but not deal with difficulties.

Effective questioning

The kinds of questions asked by teachers clearly help or discourage children's oral feedback. For detail about improving this aspect of teacher development, see *Unlocking Formative Assessment*. Recent work from the Kings/Medway Project (in Black et al., 2002) has shown that an immediate impact can be made on the quality of dialogue in the classroom if 'wait time' (the time left before children answer a question) is extended to five seconds at least. Many teachers have also tried leaving 'hands up' until the end of the wait time, or even eliminating hands up at all. This certainly raises the level of focus in the classroom! Of prime importance here is that children are given uninterrupted thinking time. The traditional classroom culture consists of brighter children answering first, often with accompanying noises or physical movements to show they have 'the answer', which stops other children dead in their thinking tracks.

Creating situations where children first discuss the answer to a question in pairs before giving feedback has valuable learning gains. Another strategy: after receiving comments from a number of children in the class, ask all the children to tell the child next to them what they would have said if they had been asked. This is very successful in releasing the words a child can often be disappointed not to be able to articulate and, of course, gives more opportunity for articulation of ideas.

Findings of the Gillingham follow-up learning team included some work on getting children to create questions, not only to promote higher-order thinking, but to make them more comfortable with questions they might be faced with. Children made up questions for each other about 3D shapes, graphs and text extracts. The process showed that they needed time and discussion to make sure they had actually written a question, and that there was enough information in the question for the recipient to be able to answer it. The project resulted in children tackling test questions more confidently and with a higher level of achievement.

Black et al. (2002), in *Working Inside the Black Box*, suggest that *'the responses that the task might evoke and the ways of following up these responses have to be anticipated'* in the planning of productive questions. Their suggestions for action in improving questioning are as follows:

- ■ *More effort has to be spent in framing questions that are worth asking (i.e. questions which explore issues that are critical to the development of pupils' understanding).*

- ■ *Wait time has to be increased to several seconds in order to give pupils time to think and everyone should be expected to have an answer and to contribute to the discussion. Then all answers, right or wrong, can be used to develop understanding. The aim is thoughtful improvement rather than getting it right first time.*

- ■ *Follow-up activities have to be rich, in that they provide opportunities to ensure that meaningful interventions that extend the pupils' understanding can take place.*

Their findings included that children became more active participants and were more readily able to understand that learning depends more on their readiness to express and discuss their own understanding than to spot the right answer.

Providing oral feedback about specific pieces of work – to children as a class, in groups or to individuals – is described in detail in the following two chapters, in which both oral and written feedback are explored within the context of a whole-school framework for feedback.

Key principles

- Oral feedback is potentially the most effective form of feedback.

- A level of challenge is a necessary prerequisite for new learning.

- Presenting difficulty as a necessary and exciting aspect of new learning, when communicated to children, leads to greater confidence and self-efficacy.

- 'Wait time' needs to be about five seconds.

- Getting children to talk together before answering questions increases their achievement.

INSET ideas

1. Present the ideas and findings about changing the language used with children when they encounter any level of difficulty. Discuss together. Ask teachers to trial this language over one week and present their findings at the next staff meeting.
2. Brainstorm self-help strategies that teachers recommend to children and share these to come up with a school list.
3. Give the staff a mental calculation to do (no talking or writing!) such as $178 - 29$ and give them one minute. Then brainstorm all the ways in which they could tell that someone had worked out the answer and what effect it had on them if they were still trying to work it out. Get them then to share how they felt when they realised that they either had the answer before the others or did not.
4. Ask teachers to trial five-second wait time, explaining to the children the importance of children having completely non-interrupted thinking time (so no eye contact, no movement, no sounds of triumph, etc) with some staff trying hands up after the five seconds and some no hands up at all. Feed back findings.
5. See *Unlocking Formative Assessment* for further INSET ideas on effective questioning.

6 A whole-school framework, rationale and policy for feedback

'Essentially it is the schools themselves that have it within their control to make substantial impact upon levels of achievement.'

(MacGilchrist, 1996)

Before exploring the different types of feedback in depth, it seems appropriate to look at all elements of feedback as a whole, forming a coherent school framework and policy. This chapter takes an 'overview' perspective, so that each piece of the jigsaw is shown to have its place and its function. The next three chapters then take the key elements of feedback in turn and explore them in depth.

The most powerful form of feedback is clearly oral, face-to-face dialogue between teacher and child, or children giving feedback to each other. Children can be taught and trained to give feedback to each other, but oral teacher–child dialogue is unmanageable in a class of 30-plus children by about Year 2 (six- and seven-year-olds). Once children generate too much work for face-to-face continuous feedback to be given, teachers have to find other ways of giving children feedback about their work. The tradition is for teachers to 'mark' the work away from the child. A number of related problem issues about feedback exist for many teachers:

Problems

1. Teachers feel that they should be marking children's work as a measure of their worth: for accountability purposes, rather than to give feedback to the child. The purpose of marking should of course be to give feedback to the child about their work.

2. Teachers feel that the quality of their feedback is measured by how much they have written on the child's work. Research shows that *too much* information is inaccessible.

3   Teachers feel that oral feedback is vital, but somehow not valid in the same way as written marking.

4   Teachers feel that even young children who cannot read the marking should have comments on their work, again to justify the feedback given to the child.

5   Teachers feel guilty if every piece of work is not marked thoroughly.

6   Teachers wonder whether their marking really makes any impact on children's progress: a soul-destroying experience.

Analyse the practice

A good starting point when working with a group of teachers, or whole staff, is to get them to brainstorm all the different types of feedback, or present them with a list. They then score the types of feedback for two things: impact on the child's learning and manageability. The discussion involved and the subsequent findings help people to realise what it is worth putting effort into and what, frankly, is no more than tradition and fear of external criticism. Creating a whole-school rationale and policy is then easier: people feel more confident about justifying their agreed practice.

The audit charts below show the outcomes of one group of teachers on one of my courses given a list of possible types of feedback (warts and all!). The rating scale is from 1 to 10, with 1 being unmanageable or little impact, and 10 being manageable and most impact. The higher the number, the more impact or the more manageable. The teachers then wrote a 'verdict' in the final column. Photocopiable versions of these charts can be found on the *Enriching Feedback* page of the Hodder website (see p. viii).

The charts are followed by a commentary (by me) about the advantages and disadvantages of the different types of feedback in terms of these findings. This could be used as part of a school 'feedback policy'.

Feedback strategies: audit

Teacher: giving written feedback

	Manageability	Impact on child's learning and progress	Verdict
Marking secretarial features (capital letters, spellings, etc), sometimes including codes.	1/2	1	Rethink and consider communication with parents, governors, etc.
Acknowledgement marking, e.g. initialled or ticked with no oral feedback.	10	0	But shows that the teacher has dealt with the work.
Acknowledgement marking after whole-class feedback.	10	8	As long as most children seem to have achieved the learning intention in some way, this is good practice, especially when the learning intention required more discussion than writing.
Summative comment relating to learning intention.	5	4/5	Not particularly worthwhile.
Highlighting success and improvement needs against the learning intention.	2	9	Persevere!
Comment on child's personal target.	5	8	Do this every now and again.
Emotional response to work.	8	0–10	Teacher's discretion, depending on child.
Comment intended for teacher's assessment or planning record.	7	0–10	Teacher's discretion, depending on child.

1 = difficult/little impact   10 = easy/high impact

Teacher: giving oral feedback

	Manageability	Impact on child's learning and progress	Verdict
Summative response, e.g. right answer.	10	2	But useful to know.
Formative dialogue, e.g. delving and questioning.	8	8	Do this.
Shared whole-class or group marking with teacher leading.	8/9	8/9	Do more of this.
Going through previously marked work with one child:			
■ Secretarial features	4	5	Limited impact.
■ Success and improvement.	6	9	Do this more.
Marking in conference with one child:			
■ Secretarial features	1/2	8	Only possible with
■ Success and improvement.	2	10	young children.

1 = difficult/little impact   10 = easy/high impact

Child marking own work

	Manageability	Impact on child's learning and progress	Verdict
Marks own closed exercises (wrong and right answers).	10	5	Saves teacher time and can be a prompt for children to sort out wrong answers.
Marks own closed exercises while teacher goes through answers and processes.	10	9	Do more of this!
Edits own work (secretarial features only).	9	8	Only if emphasis is on checking what you know is wrong rather than correcting all errors.
Identifies where personal target has been met.	8	9	Do this.
Identifies where success criteria have been achieved.	10	10	Do this.
Identifies where improvement could be made against learning intention/ success criteria and makes improvement.	10	8	Do this.

1 = difficult/little impact   10 = easy/high impact

Response partners working together

	Manageability	Impact on child's learning and progress	Verdict
Swap work and mark closed exercises.	8	1	Saves teacher time but little impact on learning.
Edit written work (secretarial features only).	8	4	Can be negative, needing many ground rules.
Identify positive aspects only.	9	8	Do this first.
Identify successes and improvement needs against learning intention.	9	9	Do this next.
Present paired marking decisions to class or group.	9	10	Aim for this.

1 = difficult/little impact   10 = easy/high impact

Commentary

Teachers' written feedback

Most time is traditionally spent marking **secretarial features** such as capital letters and full stops and punctuation, even though research shows that children's achievement is greater if the teacher's feedback focuses on the learning intention of the task. Children have many opportunities in the Literacy Hour to practise skills where the focus of the learning intention is spelling or punctuation, so we do not need to make this the focus of every piece of marking. Giving children too many criteria to focus on, and then later feedback about those criteria, causes demoralisation, puts children off writing and deters them from tackling adventurous words and keeping their focus on the learning intention of the piece. To develop specific writing expertise, learning intentions need to be precise and many pieces of writing need to be short and focused, so that aspects of writing are explored in depth (e.g. different types of cliff-hanger endings, persuasive language in a letter, etc). Any changes in emphasis in marking should be clearly communicated to parents and governors, citing research findings and explaining how spelling, etc, will be taught in places other than marking.

Acknowledgement marking, such as ticks and initials, has little impact on children's progress. However, it implies that some dialogue took place during the lesson, which will have had impact on the child's learning. The acknowledgement simply informs others that the work has been dealt with orally, in a group or whole-class setting.

A **summative comment** relating to a knowledge, skill or concept learning intention is not particularly worthwhile for children, because it usually makes them reluctant to consider any element of improvement. Those who do not attain the learning intention feel demoralised. A summative comment on an application learning intention is much more helpful, because it shows children where they have got to so far.

Highlighting success and improvement needs against the learning intention and then asking for some small improvement is rich in its impact on children's writing and their attitude to improvement and learning, but is time-consuming for teachers, especially at the beginning. This should be seen as 'quality marking' which would not take place for every piece of work. With training and modelling by the teacher, children can be encouraged to mark their own and each other's work using this approach, thus avoiding time management problems. If quality marking replaces secretarial marking, the same amount of time will be spent.

Where individual targets are used, commenting on the development of a child's personal writing target is worthwhile and manageable if it is only done occasionally. Children should be encouraged to track their own targets by tallying each time they meet it in a piece of writing, thus relieving the load for the teacher and giving children more control over their learning.

Personal, emotionally-based marking comments should be written at the teacher's discretion. Some children, especially those with special needs, seek confirmation from the teacher that they are achieving, and this can be fruitful. However, in order to aim for intrinsic motivation, we need to be sparing in our congratulations, encouraging children to identify their own successes first, then celebrating with them. *Over*-praise can produce 'praise junkies' and a dependency on the teacher's approval.

Written comments intended for **teacher's planning** rather than as feedback to the child should only be written if useful for the teacher and it should be made clear that they are not messages meant for the child to act on. However, once children can read, these could be demoralising, or at least make children feel uninvolved in the learning process.

Teachers' oral feedback

Responding to children in a whole-class setting by giving right or wrong answers is a necessary aspect of teaching, as children need to know this. However, it is only through formative dialogue (often following summative feedback) that any diagnostic, evaluative thinking will be developed. More emphasis should be put on questioning and delving, therefore.

A powerful model for marking is whole-class or group marking of one piece, with the teacher leading, but inviting children's contributions so that the piece is marked through a process of discussion, analysis and modelling. Children are more able to take ownership of marking for themselves if they have been involved in shared marking. Sessions of this kind should be worked into planning so that children can benefit from the experience on a regular basis.

Marking face to face with one child is very difficult to manage in a class setting, but is more manageable in Reception and Year 1 classes, where children do not generate so much writing at a time. However, where writing tasks continue over several sessions, it can sometimes be possible to mark alongside children. The most fruitful strategies seem to be *(a)* explaining previously marked comments which have established success and improvement against the learning intention (necessary with a few children who can't read marking comments while the rest of the class is making their improvement), or *(b)* conferencing and marking the work with the child, using the same approach but marking together. Going through secretarial features in conference with one child can also be useful, as the child has a chance to identify errors first. However, see above for warnings about demoralising and overwhelming children if there are too many errors which will not be remembered for future work.

Children marking their own work

Children marking their own closed exercises has little impact on their learning, if the reasons for their wrong answers are unknown, but is valuable in saving the teacher time. However, marking their own work while the teacher goes through the answers and processes orally can be extremely useful. It is better for a child to complete, say, only two questions but then learn more about the skill or concept during the whole-class marking, than to spend time doing more questions wrongly with no hope of finding out the right answers or the correct methods. Some misconceptions get laid down because children have practised them so many times!

Asking children to edit their own writing for secretarial features is common practice in schools, but often has limited value. If children are told to check for all spelling and punctuation errors, they are likely to be faced with a lengthy and almost impossible task of looking up words in dictionaries and finding out what they do not yet know. It is more profitable to ask children to check their work for things which they *know* are wrong. Reading aloud is especially effective in helping children identify unintended mistakes.

Getting children to take ownership of their marking is a slow process which begins with teacher modelling, shared marking and the teacher's own quality marking against the learning intention. The first step is to ask children to decide on the parts of their writing they like the most, leading to identifying success against the learning intention, then on to deciding where they could make an improvement against the learning intention.

Paired marking

As with children marking their own work, it saves teacher time if children swap exercises and mark each other's, but can be demoralising and stressful if the partner is not trusted. It is better, therefore, to allow children to mark their own work, correcting errors as they go along.

Similarly, paired children editing each other's work for secretarial features can be a merciless process unless strict ground rules are established. Looking for errors means the focus is essentially negative. Identifying, in pairs, positive aspects, then success against the learning intention, then where improvement could take place against the learning intention is more positive and will have a far greater impact on children's learning and progress. These steps need to be taken one after the other rather than all at once, so that children can thoroughly consolidate their analytical and evaluative skills as they go along.

A suggested framework for the school policy

There is clearly a need for schools to create a school policy for feedback, including marking, to provide a rationale for the different types of feedback given to children or engaged in by children.

In the following table, I suggest a framework and rationale for feedback, which can be used to create a school feedback policy. It is only when such things are spelt out and agreed by all staff as a whole-school rationale that teachers will be able to give appropriate feedback to children without guilt or fear of external criticism.

Type of feedback	Rationale
Individual oral feedback about the child's work – can be indicated by a written symbol or phrase (e.g. *'marked with child'*).	Most often used with young children where only small amounts of work are generated at a time. With older children, usually only children with special needs or those who finish work first receive this feedback.
Whole-class oral feedback.	Usually happens at the end of lessons, going through work set, talking about processes and answers, discussing and reviewing learning and any misconceptions.
Group oral feedback.	When working with a group, feedback is part of a dynamic process either at the end of or during the lesson.
Work simply ticked or initialled.	Enough oral feedback takes place during the lesson for this to be all that is required for most children to have achieved a fair level of understanding.
Closed exercises (exercises or sums requiring ticks or crosses) marked by the child while the teacher goes through each question.	It is a waste of teacher time to mark these away from children, as they have no way of knowing later why or how they made mistakes. It is more productive to give children fewer of these during the lesson, thus allowing time to go through them together while children mark and self-correct their work, thus enhancing the learning.
Quality marking by teacher.	Occasional pieces of work marked more thoroughly. The model suggested, according to research recommendations, is to focus on pointing out *success and improvement* rather than to mark every error in existence. **Concepts, skills and**

(continued)

Type of feedback	Rationale
	knowledge seem to be, on the whole, a better focus for quality written feedback, where the skill can be improved and developed, than for **application learning intentions**, which act more as a test of all the skills learnt so far.
Quality marking by children (either alone or in pairs, as response partners).	Children can gradually be trained to identify their own successes and improvement needs, with control gradually handed over from teacher to child. This then means that more pieces can be marked in this way. The feedback is many dimensional: child self-evaluation, response partner contribution and some teacher feedback.
'Test' marking for application learning intentions, where the work is an application of all skills learnt so far, providing a brief synopsis of the child's needs so far for each of the criteria: e.g. ■ spelling: you still need to watch some of your word endings, such as *-ly* and *-ion* ■ grammar: you sometimes lapse into the wrong tense — read through ■ handwriting: keep ascenders and descenders upright and parallel etc *plus* a brief comment about the overall quality of the work, and, if appropriate, a final grade.	Traditional quality marking is to take an application learning intention (e.g. a story or a whole experiment) and mark everything – spelling, all grammar, etc. It is more constructive to ask children to take account of all the criteria and then provide a synopsis. Thorough marking of spelling, etc, is more appropriate when the learning intention is about spelling.

(continued)

Type of feedback	Rationale
Combinations of the above (e.g. pointing out successes only; taking an application piece and finding one improvement point to be improved on that piece of work).	Teachers need to decide a balance between the needs of the learning intention and what is manageable. Experimenting with different ways of marking should be encouraged.
Marking every error (copy editing).	Only appropriate when the piece is to be displayed and a fair copy is needed. Children learn very little through this process, as it is carried out mechanically.
Marking against the child's target.	This is appropriate if the target was for a group and has become, in effect, the learning intention of the work. Individual targets work best in Years 4, 5 and 6, where children track their own progress. Because of this, the teacher need only comment from time to time.

In creating a school policy, it is often easier to start with some examples of other people's policies in deciding what you do and don't want for your own school. Two examples follow.

Examples of school policies for feedback

The Suffolk LEA feedback guidance includes an extract from a primary school policy for marking (reproduced from *How am I doing? – assessment and feedback to learners*, Suffolk County Council, 2001: visit www.slamnet.org.uk/assessment for details).

The second example is the whole-school marking policy developed in the course of my ongoing in-service training at Ridgeway Primary School, in Croydon.

STRATEGIES FOR MARKING
Example of a primary school approach to policy writing

Marking is only of value if comments are read and responded to/regarded.

Ideally, marking should become part of a developing dialogue resulting in pupil progress, for example; a pupil writes, the writing is marked and in her/his subsequent work, the pupil incorporates suggestions. Marking will take on a positive, rather than negative, form.

English

We need to show the children that their writing has a genuine audience, someone who is interested in what she or he has to say and is not reading their work merely to find errors. Children need to feel their writing is valued. Comments can be made verbally or in written form to communicate their message. In the case of very young children, feedback needs to be as immediate as possible.

Replying to children's work by sharing our own experience shows that the writing has a reader who is not passive but wants to share the experience and ideas. By making a pupil aware of the needs and responses of the reader, we can show her or him areas which can be developed.

We believe that correcting has its place in marking but only when it contributes to an improvement in a pupil's work. Errors need to be pointed out if a pupil is to improve her/his work; which errors and how many will depend on many factors.

We constantly assess the children's work, establishing their achievements.

Mathematics

The purpose of marking is primarily diagnostic. It will inform the day-to-day planning for the teacher. It will communicate to the child whether or not she/he is successful and will act as a motivator.

Comments will be made to emphasise the open-ended nature of mathematics and will encourage the child to feel safe when tackling problems.

Comments will reflect the stage of mathematical thinking that the child is at and will encourage further development.

Science, RE, Geography, History, Technology

Marking should be specific to skills highlighted in the lessons and subsequent follow-up work. Pupils should be able to use the comment and advice to further develop their skills. They should be helped to understand the purpose of any comments made.

Focused marking or feedback should be related to the objectives of the lesson and not necessarily based upon language and spelling.

RIDGEWAY PRIMARY SCHOOL

MARKING POLICY

This policy forms part of a whole-school policy for teaching and learning. It relates to the ethos of the school and has direct links with curriculum planning and assessment.

How children's work is received and marked and the nature of feedback given to them will have a direct bearing on learning attitudes and future achievements.

The policy must be:
- consistently applied by all staff
- clear in its purpose
- manageable
- productive in its outcomes
- informed by pupils' individual learning needs and previous assessments.

PURPOSES: Reasons for marking
- To recognise, encourage and reward children's effort and achievement, and celebrate success.
- To provide a dialogue between teacher and children and clear appropriate feedback about strengths and weaknesses in their work.
- To improve a child's confidence in reviewing their own work and setting future targets, by indicating the 'next steps' in learning.
- To indicate how a piece of work could be corrected or improved against assessment criteria.
- To help pupils develop an awareness of the standards they need to reach in order to achieve particular levels of the National Curriculum.
- To identify pupils who need additional support/more challenging work and to identify the nature of the support/challenges needed.
- To provide evidence of assessments made and help moderate the interpretation of learning intentions and levels achieved.
- To involve parents more directly in reviewing their child's progress and to help in reporting to parents.
- To aid curriculum planning.

Marking should be positive, clear and appropriate in its purpose – it needs to offer positive benefits to staff and children and the outcomes need to be fed back into planning.

(continued)

Principles

If children are to develop as independent learners, with an awareness of their own strengths as well as areas for development (learning targets) it is essential that:

■ they are made aware of the learning intentions of tasks/lessons and of the criteria against which their work will be marked/assessed. *'This is what you are going to do and this is how I will be marking it.'*

■ the learning needs of individual children are understood and work is matched and marked appropriately.

■ their work is marked in such a way that achievement is acknowledged and teaching points are highlighted.

■ where appropriate marking/feedback is linked directly to learning targets.

Wherever possible marking takes place with the children, e.g. when staff are working with a focus group. It offers guidance as to the extent to which learning intentions have been met and suggests the next steps children might take in their learning.

Towards a whole-school approach

In order to achieve a whole-school approach marking methods must be agreed and should be:

■ consistent across year groups

■ developmental across the age-range

■ consistently applied by all those working with children in school, including supply teachers and support staff.

The nature of feedback

■ Comments should refer to the learning intention of the task.

■ Comments may form the basis of a discussion between teacher and child, e.g. reviewing targets set.

■ Comments may be *oral* or *written*, formal or informal.

■ Comments may be given on a group or individual basis.

*Note: Research has shown that immediate feedback is the most effective and is therefore more likely to be **ORAL** than **WRITTEN**.*

Oral feedback ...

... is most powerful and has maximum impact when pointing out successes and improvement needs against the learning intentions. Written reflections can pull down the quality of articulation of the learning. **The quality of the thinking can be higher if it is oral.**

(continued)

... is usually interactive and developmental. It may give reassurance or a quick check on progress. The effect of teacher comments will be seen in a child's response in moving on to the next learning step.

... may be in the form of a learning/reading conference or review.

Written feedback should be

... legible and clear in meaning.

... developmental, i.e. children will find out how they are getting on and what the next learning step will be.

(It's a wasted effort if children aren't informed by it and can't progress as a result of it.)

Note: Where written feedback is used, children are expected to read comments made on their work and it is essential that time should be made available for this.

Marking at a distance

Can children read your comments?

Can they understand your comments?

Do you allow time for them to read your marking?

Do you allow time for some improvement on the work to be made before moving on to the next activity or do you expect the child to be able to transfer your improvement suggestions to another piece of work in a new context?

MARKING METHODS/CLASSROOM PRACTICE

Teachers at Ridgeway Primary School know that immediate feedback is the most effective and is therefore most likely to be oral.

CURRENT EDUCATIONAL RESEARCH SHOWS THIS TO BE SO.

General points

■ Each Autumn term year group partners should agree common marking practices and plan for a manageable amount of conference marking on a weekly basis as part of curriculum planning.

■ When written feedback is provided, time needs to be built into lessons/activity sessions for children to reflect on marking and to respond to it. This may be an interactive/questioning session.

(continued)

- Writing workshop sessions should include time for giving children feedback *including reviewing their current writing target.*
- Teachers should always mark that aspect of a pupil's work which relates to the planned learning intention. (Spelling corrections should normally be limited to words the child should know.)
- Any 'coding' or short-hand marking (e.g. initialling work to acknowledge it) should be consistent across the whole school.
- Sensitivity should always be shown towards children's work and their feelings about it and comments should be positive wherever possible. Developmental comments should be followed by a suggestion or reminder for improvement in the next piece of work.
- Use of a child's name in a written comment personalises it.
- Sharing work with the whole class or with a focus group is helpful and complements individual conferencing/target reviews.
- Self-marking/evaluation against shared learning intentions/agreed criteria can help empower a child to realise his or her own learning needs and to have control over future targets.

KEY FEATURES OF CELEBRATING ACHIEVEMENT

- Self-esteem is the most significant factor in being a successful learner.
- All achievements are linked, as each builds further confidence in future goals.
- Links between achievements should be made explicit to children.
- Children should see learning as a continuum which, given time, anyone can master.
- Achievements should be treated in exactly the same way.
- External rewards encourage children to focus on the reward rather than the achievement.
- Research shows that achievements are more effectively celebrated privately than publicly.
- Product-led Records of Achievement can reinforce lack of success for the less able.
- Develop an ethos of being able to readily identify achievements and proud moments.
- High teacher expectations can only be fulfilled with parallel measures to develop self-esteem.

Key principles

- Giving children too many criteria for writing demoralises most children – some pieces need to ask for a focus on the learning intention only.

- There needs to be a whole-school rationale for the place of different types of marking and feedback.

- There is no point in writing to a child if the child will have no means of reading or understanding it.

- Success and improvement marking enhances achievement.

- Children should be trained to gradually mark their own work, making improvements as part of a lesson.

- Paired marking enhances learning but needs training.

INSET ideas

1. After discussing the detail of the policy (see next chapters), review the current assessment or feedback marking policy in the light of staff trialling.
2. Use the photocopiable feedback audit sheets available on the *Enriching Feedback* page of the Hodder website (see p. viii) and get teachers in groups to take one aspect each, scoring as indicated. Show them the completed version afterwards and give some time for comparison and discussion. Hand out copies of the commentary (also on the website) and give time for this to be read and discussed (two staff meetings altogether). Feedback from each group should indicate which practices are worthwhile and which need review.

7 Quality feedback with young children

'The quality of dialogue in feedback is important and most research indicates that oral feedback is more effective than written feedback.'

(QCA website: www.qca.org.uk)

In the last chapter, the different types of marking were outlined and discussed, in order to create a whole-school rationale and policy. This allows teachers to more readily put their efforts into appropriate forms of feedback to match learning needs.

Quality marking is dealt with in this chapter and the next in some depth, taking a stance that the 'success and improvement' model is most appropriate if some time is to be taken over marking, rather than marking all errors. Furthermore, it seems more appropriate to focus this marking on specific taught items: *concepts, skills and knowledge*, so that the feedback encourages development of the learning, rather than on *application* learning intentions, such as writing a whole story or designing a science experiment, where more summary feedback seems appropriate.

The outline of this approach was illustrated in *Unlocking Formative Assessment*, but, since then, the strategy has been widely used throughout the UK and beyond, with at times spectacular results and reports of leaps in children's writing progress and test scores. Teachers of Years 2–6 in the Gillingham Project were asked to carry out quality marking once a week to begin with, then twice, then gradually handing over more responsibility to children in marking their work alone or in pairs using the success and improvement approach. Teachers of Reception and Year 1 were asked to use the improvement suggestions to children orally: either as they showed the teacher their work or when they interacted with them during the course of a lesson.

The results of the Gillingham Project, and the opportunity to analyse hundreds of pieces of work, have illuminated much more detail and depth about the ways in which this strategy can be used and led us to a better understanding of the possibilities for quality feedback. First of all, the approach is summarised, then children's work is used to illustrate the findings. This chapter focuses on oral feedback with younger children, and the next chapter on distance marking with children from Year 2 and above.

A summary of a 'success and improvement' strategy for marking (using all aspects orally with younger children)

1. Showing success

The teacher finds the three **best** places in the child's work which link with the learning intention and then highlights, circles or underlines these. This avoids having to write things which will be largely inaccessible to the child. All children should receive the same number. (Two successes seem more appropriate for children below Year 4, and one for Year 2 or below.) These successes should be within the context of the full ability range, so that different children could have anything from one word to a couple of sentences circled.

2. Indicating improvement

A symbol, such as an arrow, is used to indicate precisely where on the work improvement could be made (again avoiding text). The improvement is made at the end of the work.

3. Giving an improvement suggestion

An improvement suggestion is written/asked for by the teacher to help the child know how to make the specific improvement.

4. Making the improvement

Classroom time (usually first thing in the morning, the same in the afternoon or at the beginning of the next related lesson after the teacher has marked it) is given for children to read the successes and improvement suggestion and to make their improvement (typical total maximum time needed: 10 minutes). While most of the class is making the improvement, time is then generated for the teacher to read out the improvement suggestions to any children with special needs. See *Unlocking Formative Assessment* for more detail about this strategy.

In analysing many examples of teachers' marking, there appear to be three types of improvement prompts:

- the **reminder prompt** is simply a reiteration of the learning intention;

- the **scaffolded prompt** involves the teacher deciding what she would like the child to write, then finding a way of handing it back to the child;

- the **example prompt** models a choice of possible improvements, but asks if the child has an idea of his or her own.

For example, in the context of a learning intention *to be able to express characters' feelings* and the context of *a dog chasing a rabbit*, the work might look like this:

Buster's Ears pricked up at this sight of the Rabbit. A chase!

Buster ~~was~~ felt so happy on the fact that he was going to get a rabbit for his master. He would ~~see~~ surely ~~he would~~ get some fresh raw meat at supper time.

Mr. Rabbit on the other hand was not so "happy." He could be a dog's play toy for an hour or so before he was literaly scattered across the yard. Thankfully, Mr. Rabbit had a bonny PhD. in thinking quickly, so he ran for a small crevace behind the bushes. ✱

* = *Teacher's improvement prompt*
Highlighting (tinted) indicates success against the learning intention: words, phrases or sentences.

(continued)

Improvement prompts might be:

Reminder prompt
How do you think the dog felt here?

Scaffolded prompt
Describe the expression on his face.
Do you think he was annoyed? How do you think he might have shown this?
He was so surprised that he . . .
He barked _____ly, running around feeling very _____.

Example prompt
Choose one of these, or your own:
- He couldn't believe his eyes!
- He ran round in circles looking for the rabbit, feeling very confused.

Marking orally with young children

Setting the scene

Most Reception and Year 1 teachers intuitively give positive feedback or praise to young children for their efforts. We noticed in our observations in the Gillingham Project that teachers' comments tended to be evaluative (*'Good'*, *'Well done'*) and rarely reminded the child of the learning intention or described what the child had done well in relation to the learning intention.

It was often the case that the learning intentions were too broad, in the first place (e.g. *'To realise there are different types of writing'*; *'Remembering and understanding and concentrating on answering questions'*) or had too many elements (e.g. *'To produce an alternative ending to a traditional story + to be able to do a plan for the end of the story + to write down key words needed for the end of the story'*). This complexity makes it difficult to construct and phrase the feedback.

Some teachers found it difficult to give feedback focused on the learning intention and not get side-tracked into praising children for other successes or start giving feedback on other features of the work, which were unrelated to the learning intention.

In one-to-one situations **creating the right climate for feedback** emerged as an important element. When teachers opened with *'Now remember you did this wonderful piece of writing this morning…'* and read it *with* the child, they set the scene for a positive episode for children. Then children made a number of contributions to the dialogue. In contrast, opening with *'Read this to me'*, *'What have you written?'*, *'Can you remember what we are doing this work for?'* seemed like the onset of an assessment and children were noticeably more reticent.

Similarly, during guided writing sessions there was a tendency for feedback to be more about corrections than improvement, with the teacher spotting mistakes and errors as the child made them (*'Look up here – what have you missed?'*, *'What about these?… you haven't left spaces'*) and the child responding to each one as if jumping through hoops, simply reacting and probably not taking in any notion of improvement.

The nature of questioning can affect the ambience of a feedback session. Feedback sessions can have the flavour of a test when teachers ask *'What should you have put there?'* (closed) instead of *'Is there anything you think you could change to make this a proper sentence?'* or *'Oh, I wonder what could have made that a proper sentence… I wonder what's missing?'…* (open). Pausing usually encourages children to make suggestions. Open questions can encourage children to construe improvement.

It seems that Reception and Year 1 teachers either give oral feedback to children about their work after it has been finished or *during* the task, almost as a way of getting the child to produce more! Teachers tend to *(a)* sit with a child in her/his usual seat within a group but talk one-to-one, *(b)* stay in one place with children coming up to show their work from time to time, or *(c)* sit with a group of four to six and give feedback to all children as they work (usually during guided writing).

Examples of work marked orally using the 'success and improvement' model

Reminder prompts

One way of reminding a child about sentence structure is through broad hints, i.e. when a Year 1 teacher re-read part of the work aloud to the child, loudly emphasising all the 'ands' that had been used. When she then asked, *'How could you make the story flow better?'* it resulted in the child reporting **'too many "ands" – need to get rid of those "ands"'**. (To use a range of joining words had been part of the learning intention.)

Scaffolded prompts

The following types of scaffolded prompts are common:

(a) **A sentence given by the teacher with missing words**
    'A ball goes up, it always comes …?'

(b) **A specific focusing directive**
    'We could say she has yellow hair and wears…'

(c) **A specific focusing question**
    'What's the giant going to do?'
    'What happened next, did you get away?'
    'Does your friend like the present?'
    'What did the troll do when he was scared?'
    'You say the witch has peach skin … how could we make that more interesting? What could she have on her skin?'

(d) **Open-ended question/invitation**
    'Anything else? It doesn't have to be real, it can be fictional, something unusual and exciting. Something that wouldn't normally happen?'
    'How can you end your story?'

Example prompts giving two or more alternatives

'How did you feel, sad or angry?'
'Were they girls from the school or girls from next door, which?'
'What did he look like?…it would make your story more interesting…'
'What is he like? Is he tall? Thin? Short? Dumpy?'

Children's ability to act on the prompts

The power of the face-to-face teacher–child feedback scenario is one of the benefits of working with younger children. When Reception and Year 1 teachers give feedback orally one-to-one and offer prompts, children are almost always able to act – they make immediate suggestions or write something down.

Example (Y1 have been trying to use adjectives to clearly describe a 'Wanted' criminal so people would recognise him/her.)

Teacher: *'You say the witch has got peach skin. How could we make that more interesting? What could she have on her skin?'*
Child: **'Burns.'**
Teacher: *'How did she get them?'*
Child: **'When she went to sleep, some people came in and burnt her.'**
Teacher: *'So I could put here "The witch has burns on her skin". That gives more detail... now I think I could find her from your description.'*
[Here the teacher specifies why her question has led to an improvement (*'That gives more detail'*) in relation to the learning intention (*'Now I think I could find her from your description'*)].

As a way of reminding children of their successful improvements, Reception and Year 1 teachers often wrote down the improvements children had expressed verbally.

Example (A Y1 boy was writing sentences to go with a set of pictures.)

Child reads his sentences: **'Rags was in his basket trying to go to sleep. The cat tickled Rags. Rags woke up with one eye and peeked at the cat.'**
Teacher: *'What do you think Rags will do?'*
Child: **'He made a mean face.'**
Teacher writes: *'What do you think Rags will do?'* on the work and **while she is quiet, the child adds more:**
Child: **'He made a mean face and chased the cat.'**
Teacher writes child's words on the work and says *'I like that.'*

Overall, although Reception and Year 1 children nearly always offer something in response to prompts, they are often 'just answering the teacher' rather than engaging with how their suggestion improves their work, *unless* the teacher specifies why her question and the child's answer leads to an improvement (*'What did he look like? It would make your story more interesting…'*).

In the Gillingham observations, when Reception and Year 1 teachers highlighted successes (or stressed them verbally), children often responded by showing the teacher another success.

Examples
(a) Reception teacher: *'You did this so well … you tried to sound out "horse" and "rabbit".'*
Child: **'And I did that one!'** (pointing to 'cat').

(b) Reception teacher: *'That's very good. You've put a "t" in. What else do you have?'* (encouraging self-assessment).
Child: **'An "A" for ark.'**

When teachers highlighted successes in relation to the learning intention and combined it with a question to scaffold understanding, children stuck to the learning intention in their response.

Example (The learning intention for a Y1 child was to produce text to go with a 'Wanted' poster – to describe the character so people would recognise him/her.)

Teacher: *'Now let's read your description.'*
Child and teacher read: **'He is small and handsome and his buttons are made of strawberries.'**
Teacher: *'Strawberry buttons. Lovely and he's small and handsome. … What else could we say about him?'*
Child: **'He is greedy.'**

Complete examples of work marked orally

Fig. 1

Figure 1 shows the work of a first-term Reception child, in response to the learning intention *'**To list what a pet needs**'*. The text reads:

1. I like my puppy.

2. I like to play with my puppy.

3. I will look after my puppy.

The teacher told the child one success: *'Well done – you've said you will look after your puppy.'* She then asked the child: *'How will you look after your puppy?'* The child's oral response was *'By giving it some food and water.'* He then sat down and wrote these words. Interestingly, because the context has been muddled with the learning intention, the teacher was more focused on the pet than the list-making. We might argue that the most successful element of the piece, according to the learning intention, was the numbers of the layout of a list. Similarly, if the focus had been on the list, the improvement would have probably been to write a number 4 for another statement.

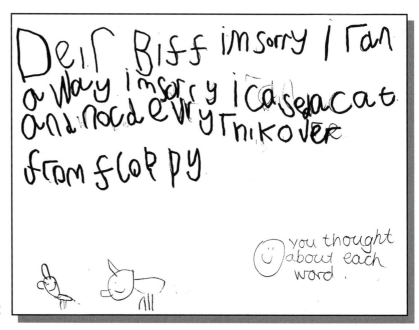

Fig. 2

Figure 2 shows the work of a Year 1 child, in response to the learning intention *'Think about the beginning sounds of the words before you write them down'*. The class was involved in a literacy lesson, and one group was writing letters. The teacher sat with another group a lot of the time, but circulated regularly. On one of these trips, she talked to each child on the letter-writing table about their work, informing them in advance that they would be told two successes and one place to improve. The text reads:

> Dear Biff,
>
> I'm sorry I ran away. I'm sorry I chased a cat and knocked everything over.
>
> From Floppy

The teacher praised the child for the 'fr' in *from* and the 'fl' in *Floppy* and then chose the word *chased* for the improvement. She asked the child to read that bit again, remembering the beginning sounds (a reminder prompt), and, in reading it, he spotted the error and self-corrected. If he had not done this, she would have had to use a scaffolded prompt (e.g. *'The word chased is not quite right. Do you know any other words that begin with the "ch" sound?'*) or maybe an example prompt (e.g. *'The word chased is spelt like this. Let's think of some other words that begin with the "ch" sound.'*)

Impact on children's writing

Teachers reported that some Reception children did not have the concentration to make the improvement there and then. So they would tell them what the next step would be, then be sure to reinforce that before children started the next bit of writing. However, some Reception children could 'hold oral feedback in their heads' and independently apply it to subsequent writing. Overall their writing showed improvements in structure, content and imagination. More able Year 1 children were reported to 'have more ideas'.

'Yes using the strategy orally is making an impact on children's writing. I've noticed they're getting more writing done and their sentence structure is better, because they're released from spelling. There's more flow in their writing.' (Reception teacher)

'I think it is extending children's vocabulary, they think of other words. Now they are reading back through their work and writing some more, not just giving work in.' (Y1 teacher)

'The able children can see where they can add something e.g. more description, and can see the improvement.' (Reception teacher)

Vignettes showing ways of using the oral feedback strategy

The following examples demonstrate feedback interaction between teachers and Reception and Year 1 children in full. They illustrate many of the points made in this section.

Tom

After a Year 1 class lesson about different excuses for being late for school, Tom had been asked to write a story, explaining clearly what had happened and why he was late.

The teacher had read his work and explained, *'I can see why you were late* (highlighting success), *but not what happened exactly'* (referring to where improvement was needed to meet the learning intention).

Tom explained: *'Some girls kissed me.'*
The teacher gave two example prompts: *'Were they girls from the school or girls from next door to you? Which?'*
'From school,' replied Tom and wrote spontaneously, *'and they came from the school'.*

Arabella

The Reception teacher had been encouraging children to understand that writing needs to be understood by someone reading it. She looked at Arabella's writing about what she had done at the weekend. Large figure drawings dominated the page and in inch-high writing (somewhat carelessly formed) Arabella had written:

'This is meyand nany and *m u m* and *grandadad* and Ben weare atthe pub. I wach the teveyison of mey dansin.'

The teacher asked, kindly, *'Oh, Arabella, can you read this?'*
'No,' said Arabella.
'So how can we improve this, Arabella?' the teacher probed.
'Make it neater, smaller and put in spaces,' said Arabella.

The teacher wrote *'Make it neater, smaller and put in spaces'* at the top of the next blank page and Arabella proceeded to make the improvements. Her writing was even-sized, smaller and there were finger spaces between words. Arabella added her own smiley face to the work.

'Can you read this now?' asked the teacher.
'Yes,' said Arabella and proceeded to read her news aloud.

Later Arabella showed the researcher her Sounds Book, pointing out another improvement she had made earlier. *'I wrote all scribbly over those words. By not writing over words, I could make them easier to read so I wrote them out again.'*

Poppy

Year 1 children were required to provide a sample of work for their profiles. The learning intention was that the story had a beginning, a middle and an end. Poppy had written her story (quite independently) the day before the teacher gave her feedback. Feedback was given when the other children had begun their morning's work. The teacher invited Poppy to sit beside her on the armchair and put her arm around her.

After Poppy had read her story to the teacher and they had shared a few highlights and laughs on the way…

Teacher: 'That was a FANTASTIC story with such details in it. [Pauses] Then … all of a sudden it ends!' [Reads out the ending] 'so she ran away.' That was really sudden, wasn't it?'

Poppy: [Nods]

Teacher: 'What happened just before that?'

Poppy: [Retells that bit of the story]

Teacher: 'What could you do if you had more time? I think I might have [modelling example prompts] been very frightened, might have opened my eyes wide – very scared, might have run away very fast. What would you do if you had more time?'

Poppy: 'I'd write: "She ran straight away. She ran and ran and ran and she never went there again!"'

Key principles

■ Teachers' oral feedback needs to be focused mainly around the learning intention of the task.

■ Learning intentions need to be focused to be useful for feedback.

■ Young children need a nurturing climate when talking about their work.

■ Teachers need to say explicitly what the child could do to improve the work, or the child simply answers the teacher's questions.

INSET ideas

1. Make sure that learning intentions in short-term plans are specific knowledge, skills, concepts or applications. Teachers in pairs could have a go together at this.
2. Brainstorm the language used when talking to children about their writing.
3. Pairs can observe each other giving feedback to individuals, keeping notes about the impact of their language and body language. They then compare notes and discuss implications.
4. Get any principles and action written into school policy, so that new practice is validated and has more chance of remaining in place.

8 Quality feedback through marking

'Marking is usually contentious but often fails to offer guidance on how work can be improved. In a significant minority of cases, marking reinforces under-achievement and under-expectation by being too generous or unfocused.'

(OfSTED, 1996)

Marking against learning intentions

One of the first issues to emerge in talking to teachers about the 'success and improvement' marking strategy outlined in the previous chapter was the importance of a clear learning intention, or a specific knowledge, concept or skill, rather than a broad learning intention like *'To write an effective poem'* or *'To write a story'*. Finding successes in the latter can be difficult, as there are too many criteria to be taken into consideration. With a specific focus, the task is much simpler. Having success criteria also makes the task much more manageable, because the success criteria help the teacher (and child) know what to look for when highlighting success.

Some examples of learning intentions in Literacy which would be appropriate for the 'success and improvement' approach:

■ *To write a mystery story, using mysterious phrases and suspense.*

■ *Plan/write a persuasive letter.*

■ *To use effective adjectives in a story/to complete a story.*

■ *Put adjectives in front of nouns to produce exciting description.*

■ *To use a previous description within a story.*

■ *To describe characters as a retelling.*

■ *To show the characteristics of a person's character by inference.*

■ *To write a traditional story changing one of the characters.*

Analysing the marking

I have been lucky enough to analyse hundreds of examples of children's writing, across the curriculum, which have been marked using the success and improvement model. The following section looks at different types of improvement prompts and how they have impacted on children's subsequent improvement.

Whether framed as a reminder prompt, a scaffolded prompt or an example prompt, teachers' improvement suggestions generally fall into the following categories:

1   Elaborating and extending (*'tell us more...'*)

2   Adding a word or sentence (*'add one word...'*)

3   Changing the text (*'find a better word'*)

4   Justifying (*'why...?'*)

In order to give many practical examples of improvement suggestions and children's responses, I have faithfully copied the child's text rather than shown the entire piece each time. At the end of this section, a few original whole pieces of writing have been reproduced. Whenever children's quotes are included, their Year and broad ability grouping (above average, average and below average) are indicated. We asked teachers to choose children for interview from the middle of these three ability ranges.

1. Elaborating and extending

Reminder prompts for elaborating or extending

Some teacher prompts act as a '**reminder**' and simply redirect the child's attention to the learning intention of the task as a way of focusing the improvement. This device seems most appropriate for brighter children, who need less support in making their improvements. For instance:

'Write a character description of James.'
'Describe the merman.'
'Say more about the fire.'
'Explain this for me.'

Scaffolded prompts for elaborating or extending

Scaffolded prompts tended to either *(a) focus the child's attention on specifics* or *(b) delve via two or more questions or statements.* This is generally supportive unless too many questions are asked, giving children too many things to think about. The following examples produced improvements which the teachers considered had enhanced the child's original writing. The child's written improvement is shown each time.

(a) Focusing on specifics

Learning intention: To include detail.
Text extract:

A moment later Katie landed in a smelly muddy jungle. She saw a loin, she smelled a snake's breath.

What did the snake's breath smell of?

The snakes' breath smelt of rotten eggs. (Above-average Y2)

Learning intention: To write a paragraph which uses suspense.
The teacher in this instance had asked children to identify the place they would improve, so the child chose a sentence to elaborate, by marking it with asterixes:

Suddenly there was a cry the sherpas had fallen. Stuart saw them hit the floor.

Could you put a little more suspense into the climbing of the mountain?

His improvement:

Stuart heard a shriek because he could hear the people at the bottom. This could mean anything, it could mean someone at the bottom was in trouble. The only things going through his head was danger. He spun round. He couldn't see anything bad. Where were his sherpas. He looked down. They had plunged head first and hit their heads and died.
(Above-average Y6)

Learning intention: To use similes and metaphors to describe different aspects of the night.
Text extract:

Cautiously I edged back to my deserted tent and sat waiting for the morning to come.

Describe what the deserted tent looked like to you as you approached it.

Cautiously I edged back to my deserted tent, deserted like a hollow beehive, abandoned by every living insect that passed, and sat waiting for the morning to come. (Above-average Y6)

(b) Delving

Learning intention: To write exciting sentences from notetaking.
Entire text:

Daniel is energetic and has a character with lots of hobbies. His favourite sports are cricket, golf and football. He likes them because it is his style. It is his style because he likes watching it and playing them. Daniel would like to play for Man U or play in the cricket tournament.

Can you tell me more about why Daniel enjoys his hobbies? Why does he want to play in the competitions?

Daniel would like to play in these competitions because he wants to be famous. He wants to be famous because he wants to live a good life. He knows that if he wants his dreams to come true he will have to work hard. (Above-average Y5)

Learning intention: To write an effective description.
Text extract:

There was penguins everywhere, the penguins are white with black wings. They are about half a metre long.

Tell us more. What do they look like? How do they move?

They have a yellow beak with white on the inside of the wings and black on the outside. They cant fly but can swim very fast and don't run but wodle. (Average Y4)

Learning intention: To write a given story from the point of view of one of the characters.
Text extract:

I was glad that old daniel took over dicks job. He really loves horses and so do I.

How do you treat the horses? Write about times you have anything to do with the horses.

I treat the horses like their my family so I guess I treet them as loving caring horses. I like the times when I rode on black beauty and the others. I also liked when I am giving them their tea seeing their happy smiles and I also like seeing them cheerful inside. (Below-average Y6)

Example prompts for elaborating or extending

Teachers sometimes ask children to elaborate their descriptions by giving them models of words or phrases they might use: an **example prompt**. This is most often used for younger children or children who needed more specific support in making an improvement. Although children often take one of the examples offered, many children also appear to be stimulated to think of their own alternative, as in the second example.

Learning intention: To write an effective description.
Text extract:
Then the umbrella started to drop it dropped lower and lower.

Describe what you are seeing as you drop lower and lower. Perhaps

- *Cars look like toys*

- *Houses look like dolls' houses*

- *People look like ants*

I saw cars looking like toys and people like ants (Below-average Y3)

Learning intention: To write an effective description.
Text extract:
I went on a boat and went long on water

What did you see on the boat trip? Fish? Birds? People?

I see a jellyfish and carb (crab). (Below-average Y4)

Learning intention: To retell a given story.
Text extract:
Mr Gumpy made some dine and they eat some and they made a mese erey were (made a mess everywhere)

What mess did they make? Tick one of these

- ☐ *They kept throwing food on the floor.*

- ☐ *They kept talking with their mouths open.*

- ☐ *They ran around the room.*

(This below-average Y3 child ticked the first box.)

2. Adding a word or sentence

Another popular improvement suggestion is to ask the child to add a word or sentence to the existing text. The prompt is usually written in a very structured way. In many cases, these improvement suggestions are simply a different way of asking the child *Why?* or *What?* questions, but, because of their supportive structure, produce better written responses.

When asking for an extra word or sentence, teachers tend to:

(a) provide a format for children to write directly into (e.g. finishing a sentence or filling in missing words);

(b) ask for one or two new words, usually an adjective;

(c) ask for one or two sentences with a specific instruction.

(a) Providing a format

Missing words

With this device, the teacher writes a sentence leaving words or parts of words missing, to support the child's thinking and sentence structure.

Learning intention: To use adjectives and adverbs.
Text extract:

The Argonauts set a trap wiel Jason was trying to derstack him but the dragon was to strong and he got past

Let's use some adverbs to describe how they fought.

Jason tried <u>in vain</u> to distract him, but the dragon <u>vishesly</u> used his strength to get past. Jason stabbed his sword <u>quickly</u> into the dragon's nearest side. (Below-average Y5)

Finishing the teacher's beginning

Many teachers start the child off with a phrase or sentence, for example:

Learning intention: To use effective similes and metaphors.
The teacher has linked the prompt to the child's work:

A quick runner

As fast as *<u>a cheater</u>* (Below-average Y3)

(b) Asking for one or two new words

Learning intention: To use effective adjectives.
Text extract:

The next time he shouted wolf they did not come and this time there was a wolf

Emma, think of a really good adjective to describe the wolf

A blud sucking turerfeing wolf (Average Y3)
(A blood-sucking terrifying wolf)

Learning intention: To use effective adjectives.
Text extract:

He was horifide of the woodcutter because he has a axe.

Use an adjective to describe the axe, like an enormous axe, a sharp axe, a gleaming axe.

The woodcutter had a gleaming axe. (Average Y3/4)

(c) Asking for one or two sentences

More specific and structured than elaboration, many teachers ask for only one or two sentences, often for young or below-average children.

Learning intention: To use rhyming words (own version of The Owl and the Pussycat)
Text extract:

The shark with its jaws was ready to devour,

The owl and the pussycat was shivered under a coat

Think of a line to rhyme with devour.

The owl was scared to use its power (Average Y4)

Learning intention: To describe a character.
Text extract:

Tim was a good boy and hes brom hais it was spikey but Tim saw quiet and bright intelligent eyes.

Can you tell me two things Tim likes doing?

Tim likes doing is collecting isecs and wochin the ciyos chanol (Below-average Y3)
(Tim likes doing is collecting insects and watching the science channel)

Learning intention: Retell a traditional story.
Text extract:

...and there was the mermaid just standing there and they went home and lived happerly ever after.

What did the mermaid say to the merman before they went home together?

You will allways be my frend. (Average Y2)

3. Changing the text

A further, frequently used improvement suggestion is asking the child to change the existing text in some way, replacing individual words, a sentence or two or paragraphs. All three styles of prompts (reminder, scaffolded and example) can be used.

(a) Replacing individual words

The first example here is interesting because it shows the apparent impact of taking the same learning intention for two consecutive pieces of work. The adjectives used in the first piece (*purple* and *smelly*) were inserted by the child as the result of a final reminder about the learning intention at the end of the lesson. Two more adjectives are added as a result of the teacher's improvement suggestion. By contrast, the second piece is significantly improved, probably because of both the continued focus and the positive impact of the marking strategy.

Learning intention: To use effective adjectives.
Child's first piece
Entire text:

I went to Cornwall we went to the beach and we found a porple starfish. My mum found some shrimps and they were smelly. We went to the dolphin club and we played <u>games</u> and danced and I found a twenty pound note in a crisp packit and I slpet on a <u>cowch</u> with my brother

You used two adjectives. Look at the two words I have underlined. Can you add adjectives to describe these things – e.g. fun games, lumpy old couch or think of your own? (**fun** and **big** then inserted by child)

Child's second piece
Entire text:

On a sunny day I went to the funfair. I went on an exciting ride. It had old ladys and men. It was a dark ride. I went on a good ride first. It gos slowley and then it gos fast. I went in this sort of hansle and gretle skary house. There was a ball pit. It was very dark. It was a big house and a big ball pit.

Brilliant adjectives. Can you think of a better adjective than 'big'? You could try large, enormous, huge … or one of your own.

It was an enormous house and a massive ball pit. (Above-average Y2)

The next piece also shows the development with consecutive pieces of work. In the first piece (not shown) the child wrote the beginning and middle of a story, using dialogue, but only ever using the word 'said'. The child is asked to meet the improvement suggestion in the following day's work, which is the continuation of the story.

Learning intention: To use effective dialogue.
Very good start. Count how many times you have used 'said'. What might you have used instead?

Extract from follow-up piece:
'Yes I am' pronounced Mr James 'and I will deal with you later'.
'What was all that about' exclaimed his wife.
'Nothing really' grumbled Captain Birds Eye.
'I had to say something important to you' said his wife, worried. 'When I was going to do something to eat I was going to cook sausage sandwichs and I couln't because the sausages had disapeared completely, not one left.'
'Well, I will have to go and buy some then shouldn't I' admitted captain birds eye.
'The shops are shut' answered his wife. (Below-average Y6)

(b) Replacing individual sentences

Learning intention: To understand genre (cowboy story) and continue a piece in suitable style, using appropriate words and phrases.

Text extract:
Tex was trailing through Tombstone when he saw the Clancy gang.
'Hay, Clancy gang, this town ain't big enough for the 2 of us. I'll give you till sundown to get your puney butts outta town.' Said Tex. <u>The gang road off on their horses.........</u>

You have understood the genre well. Can you think of a better way of writing this sentence?

The gang galloped away on their horses cowardly (Average Y6)

Learning intention: To take notes.
Original text:

The Himalayas and the other ranges of mountains take one sixth of India.
India has the most beautiful valleys.
In India the temperatures rise.

You have chosen three interesting facts. You do not need to write them in sentences here, just notes, e.g. valleys, most beautiful.
Cut down this information to just two words: Tropics – spring is the hottest time of the year.

Spring hottest (Below-average Y5)

(c) Replacing paragraphs

A common improvement suggestion is to ask the child to replace an existing paragraph altogether. More often than not this is the last paragraph of the piece, probably indicating that the child has run out of time and/or steam! It is also likely that teachers spend more time teaching children about story openings than endings.

Learning intention: To write a story with an effective beginning, middle and end.

Text extract:
The trap door opened slowly. William was seen, but looking at me, sternly. Then, he faded into a grey puff of smoke.

I'm not quite sure what happens at the end of this story. Please could you explain it below.

William rises on the platform. He looks at James as if he had been taken over by the phantom. A puff of smoke raised into the air in front of William. By the time the smoke had disappeared, William was nowhere to be seen! (Above-average Y6)

Interestingly, the child has picked up the teacher's use of the present tense, which puts the first two sentences into the wrong tense. It is also common to see the child apparently writing directly to the teacher, rather than creating an improved ending, when the teacher's prompt is phrased in this personal way. A better prompt would be, perhaps, *'I'm not quite sure what happens at the end of this story. Please rewrite the ending, explaining what happens in more detail.'*

The next example shows both highlights and an improvement marked independently **by the child**. The whole piece is shown, so that the child's choice of success (underlined sections) can also be shown.

Learning intention: To write an effective ending to a story.

Entire text:

Moonfleet ending

The cold, deep voices of the smuglers echoed on the rocky, damp walls surrounding me. My pounding heart thumped as hard as the smuglers footsteps, determind to approch this musky, lonely coffin like the rabbit again, trapped. My mind started to wander away seeing Cracky Jones dead on the frosty grass, me dead on the grass or the more painful picture <u>my babling toung stilled, my prying eyes sealed.</u>

<u>Smuglers voices grew louder and red hot torches flickered harder</u> when footsteps came rushing down the staires. Twas the vicar who stumbled into the vault. His scared eyes calmed as he saw the man but not for long. The younger man crept towards him with anger in his eyes a silver shine gleamed out of his hand the two very different expressioned eyes met.

<u>The sheer sight made my eyes trickel</u>. The red gashes spread across the floor the screams echoed through every wall, everything. I couldn't bear it the services he had held the people he had healed he was now dead.

The men began to talk of what to do with the body it had been decided it was going in this spot. I felt shocked what was I going to do now? I couldn't get away from them. Unless....

As they turned to drag the beer belly vicar I scrambled into the old rotten wooden coffin. My breath grew deeper as I turned to the dead man lying next to me you never guess what I saw a huge shiny diamond....

The last paragraph was crossed out by the child and replaced with:

As they turned to drag the beerbelly vicar I scrambled into the old rotten wooden coffin. My breath grew deeper as I turned to the dead man's face. I felt an uncomfortable object on my side. I shuffled and there, lying there was a huge shiny diamond... (Above-average Y6)

4. Justifying

The last most popular improvement suggestion is to ask the child to justify something from the text, always expressed as a *Why?* question (a scaffolded prompt). Although children's responses are usually enthusiastically written, children often write directly to the teacher, as if to explain something she clearly had not understood, rather than writing the improvement as if it were still part of the text. Training the children with the strategy is the key here – all of the pieces shown in this chapter were generated within the first few weeks of children being introduced to this way of marking. Each example has the potential to make a significant improvement to the original text. It would probably be more productive to add the word *'because…'* to the original text, so that the child is encouraged to continue in the same style, within the story genre. Alternatively, the child could be asked to rewrite the original sentence, including the reasons.

Learning intention: To continue a story in the same style.
Text extract:

Mr Fox said 'are you all right' in a shakie voice.

Why was his voice shaky…? Tell me more!

Mr Fox's voice was shaky because lady mary had fainted and he was scared because he didn't want to lose the one he loved and he didn't want her dead because he didn't want to be killed himself. (Average Y5)

Learning intention: To write the beginning of a story sequel.
Text extract:

Cinderella's ugly sisters were jealous of her so they made plans to ruin the wedding.

Why were the ugly sisters jealous of Cinderella?

Because the prince loved her not them. They were also jealous of Cinderella because she was more beuatiful then them. (Above-average Y3)

> *Learning intention: To write a story with an effective beginning, middle and end*
> Text extract:
>
> It was obvious to me that they had never seen a human before.
>
> *Why was it obvious to you?*
>
> The reason it was obvious to me was because they looked puzzled when I enterd their planet. And it looked as if they were trying to work out what planet I came from. Because they looked as if they didn't know what type of spices I was. They also looked a bit scared. I guessed this was practicly because they had never seen a human before.
> (Above-average Y4)

Classroom management

Alternative ways of giving improvement suggestions

Once children understand the significance and the purpose of circling or highlighting successes and improvements, they rarely object to the apparent 'defacing' of their work. In fact, they want to know where their successes are if they don't appear! However, when the work is to be displayed as fair copy, clearly the piece should remain unblemished. The Suffolk LEA guidance on marking suggests that with ongoing, more complex pieces of work, some teachers have used 'Post-it' notes or 'wrap-arounds'. Children keep the Post-it notes on the back page of their books. Some schools use Post-it notes with response partners (i.e. children read their partner's work and then say on a Post-it note two ways they could improve it).

Using the strategy in other subject areas

Clearly, any subject in which there is prose lends itself to the success and improvement strategy. The learning intention is still the focus, so, as long as that is clear, the strategy should work. If the activity is too closed (e.g. wrong or right answers required), the strategy is not the best vehicle for feedback (see Chapter 6 for advice about closed exercises).

Some teachers use the strategy for mathematics, by using the improvement prompt either for a wrong answer or, if there are no wrong answers, as an extension prompt.

Figures 3 and 4 show Year 6 mathematics and then history in which the strategy has been applied. The learning intentions are *'To be able to make predictions and use a spread sheet to test them'* and *'To understand the significance of the River Nile in Ancient Egypt'*

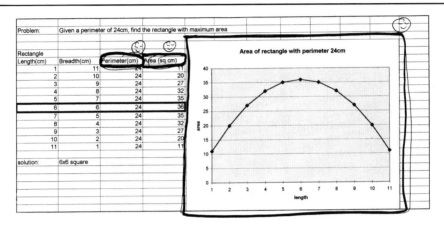

Problem:	Given a perimeter of 24cm, find the rectangle with maximum area		
Rectangle Length(cm)	Breadth(cm)	Perimeter(cm)	Area (sq.cm)
1	11	24	11
2	10	24	20
3	9	24	27
4	8	24	32
5	7	24	35
6	6	24	36
7	5	24	35
8	4	24	32
9	3	24	27
10	2	24	20
11	1	24	11
solution:	6x6 square		

Learning intention: To be able to make predictions and use a spreadsheet to test them.

Success criteria: that you use a spreadsheet, using formulae to calculate totals in cells, and use the graphs tool to create a graph to help you answer the problem.

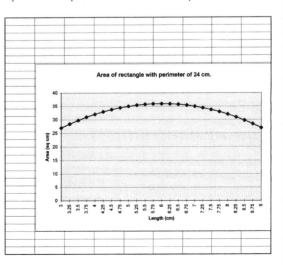

Problem:	Given a perimeter of 24 cm, find the rectangle of maximum area				
Rectangle Length(cm)	Breadth(cm)	Perimeter(cm)	Area (sq.cm)	Length(cm)	Area (sq.cm)
3	9	24	27	3	27
3.25	8.75	24	28.4375	3.25	28.4375
3.5	8.5	24	29.75	3.5	29.75
3.75	8.25	24	30.9375	3.75	30.9375
4	8	24	32	4	32
4.25	7.75	24	32.9375	4.25	32.9375
4.5	7.5	24	33.75	4.5	33.75
4.75	7.25	24	34.4375	4.75	34.4375
5	7	24	35	5	35
5.25	6.75	24	35.4375	5.25	35.4375
5.5	6.5	24	35.75	5.5	35.75
5.75	6.25	24	35.9375	5.75	35.9375
6	6	24	36	6	36
6.25	5.75	24	35.9375	6.25	35.9375
6.5	5.5	24	35.75	6.5	35.75
6.75	5.25	24	35.4375	6.75	35.4375
7	5	24	35	7	35
7.25	4.75	24	34.4375	7.25	34.4375
7.5	4.5	24	33.75	7.5	33.75
7.75	4.25	24	32.9375	7.75	32.9375
8	4	24	32	8	32
8.25	3.75	24	30.9375	8.25	30.9375
8.5	3.5	24	29.75	8.5	29.75
8.75	3.25	24	28.4375	8.75	28.4375
9	3	24	27	9	27

Fig. 3

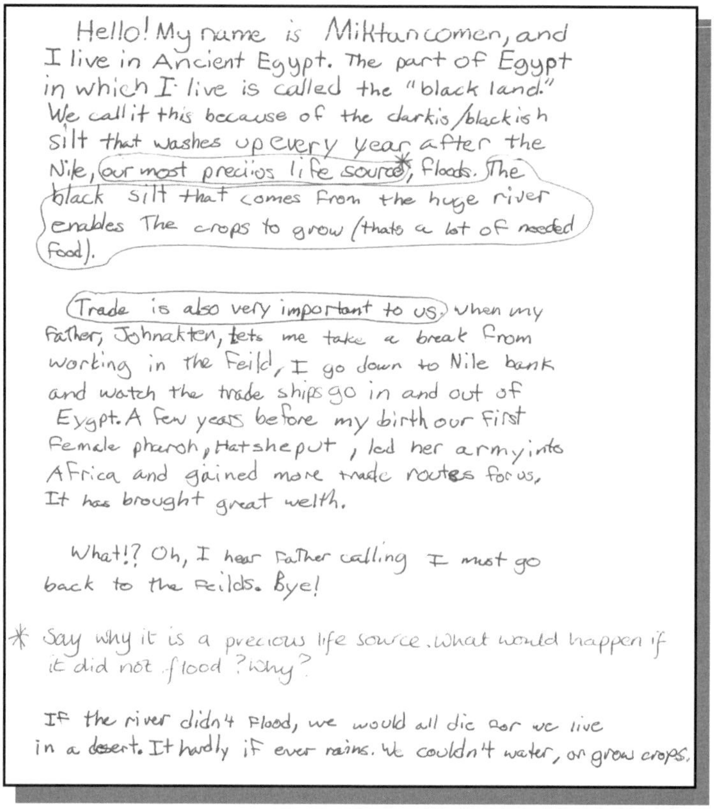

> Hello! My name is Miktancomen, and I live in Ancient Egypt. The part of Egypt in which I live is called the "black land." We call it this because of the dark is/blackish silt that washes up every year after the Nile, our most precious life source, floods. The black silt that comes from the huge river enables the crops to grow (thats a lot of needed food).
>
> Trade is also very important to us. When my Father, Johnakten, lets me take a break from working in the Feild, I go down to Nile bank and watch the trade ships go in and out of Eygpt. A few years before my birth our first Female pharoh, Hatsheput, led her army into Africa and gained more trade routes for us, It has brought great welth.
>
> What!? Oh, I hear Father calling I must go back to the Feilds. Bye!
>
> * Say why it is a precious life source. What would happen if it did not flood? Why?
>
> If the river didn't flood, we would all die aor we live in a desert. It hardly if ever rains. We couldn't water, or grow crops.

Fig. 4

The next chapter shows a piece of peer-marked science in which the 'success and improvement' model was used.

To avoid foundation subjects being marked for literacy skills only, many schools focus on the subject-specific vocabulary and give these to children, ask for these spellings to be correct and sometimes test children on these lists. This then allows more focus to be applied to the subject learning intention.

Training the children

Teachers have found the easiest and quickest way of introducing children to this marking strategy is to use a piece of writing from another class and copy it onto acetate. Go through the work on an overhead projector, pointing out the learning intention, reading it through, finding the successes together, etc, so that the strategy is discussed as a whole-class activity. This is a useful thing to do every now and again, because you can then engage in a dialogue with the class about the reasons for the successes, which would be too time-consuming if the work were distance-marked.

Teachers of Year 2 and Year 3 sometimes say it is better to start by setting children off in groups during guided writing sessions, so that they really understand the strategy.

From as early as Year 2, children can be trained to look for successes and improvements themselves. This is dealt with in the next chapter.

The learning intention as the title?

Many teachers have found there is an expectation that learning intentions appear on children's work, so that all stakeholders are aware of its context. This can be very time-consuming for both teachers and children. Abbreviating the learning intention to as few words as possible, as the title of the work, seems the best strategy. For example

To be able to use effective adjectives becomes **Adjectives**.

To be able to make predictions and use a spread sheet to test them becomes **Predictions and spread sheets**.

To know what a pharaoh is and to understand their importance in Ancient Egypt becomes **Pharaohs**.

The links between targets and marking

Over the last few years, there has been a gradual shift from specific individual writing targets to the more manageable use of group targets. The Gillingham research concluded that for foundation stage children social targets seem best; for children up to about Year 4 group targets work well; and for the remaining years at least two approaches are possible:

1 Children create their own individual targets from given lists of criteria, track these and consult the teacher where necessary.

2 Children receive a list of the current coverage for, say, Literacy, and keep a more global eye over where they think they are doing well and where they need to put more effort.

There were several **negative** findings about the use of individual targets:

■ The learning intentions of lessons often do not give children the opportunities to fulfil or practise their target.

■ Children usually understand their target but often have no idea about how to achieve it.

■ The amount of effort required by teachers in order to keep track of every child's target is out of all proportion to the impact they have on children's writing.

Because of these factors, I favour the second strategy above, in which children look over a list of targets rather than being confined to one very specific target for any number of weeks.

Where individual targets exist, children seem able to understand the difference between the learning intention of today's lesson and their longer-term, context-free target. Marking the child's target for every piece of work would be overkill (for teachers and children), so it seems best to comment only when some change has taken place or something significant needs to be pointed out. Individual targets are still often used for children with special needs or for those with behavioural problems.

What can go wrong!

There is a steep learning curve for teachers after the first batch of work marked in this way is returned, complete with children's improvements. It is then that you realise how effective your improvement suggestion actually was. Figure 5 shows an example of a child's response which illustrates the need for a more structured improvement prompt – perhaps an example prompt – giving different possibilities.

The improvement suggestion needs to be more direct, using words like 'State...', 'Where would be....?', 'Suggest...', etc.

However, this piece is useful in demonstrating that the question itself might be inappropriate. If we consider the land around the school and where to put 20 houses, there is a basic problem that all the land is used. It is important to put yourself in the child's shoes and imagine what you would write. Perhaps a better question would be *'If you could demolish something around the school which is not being usefully used, what would it be and why?'*

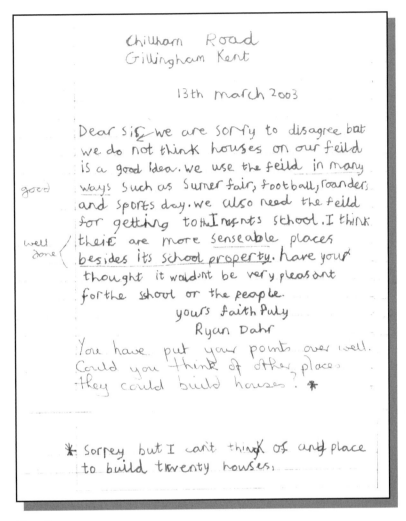

Fig. 5

Complete examples of children's writing

After examples of a range of reminder, scaffolded and example prompts, the following pages contain entire pieces of children's writing, complete with learning intention, highlighted success, improvement prompts and children's subsequent improvement. They serve to demonstrate many of the examples analysed in this section.

Improvement prompts

Range of prompts	Learning intention	Extract from child's writing	Reminder prompt
Why...? (justifying a statement)	To write a letter giving reasons for things you say.	'It was dismal.'	Say why you thought this.
How did you/s/he feel?	To retell a story showing people's feelings.	'Nobody believed him.'	Say how you think this made him feel.
Add something	To use effective adjectives and adverbs in an account.	'Jason was trying to distract him, but the dragon was too strong.'	Use more adverbs and adjectives here.
Change something	To use effective adjectives in a description.	'He was a bad monster.'	Think of a better word than *bad*.
Tell us more	To introduce a character in a story opening.	'James went to school.'	Could you describe James?
What happens next?	To write a middle and end from a given start.	'At last the merman saw the mermaid.'	How is your story going to end?

Scaffolded prompt	Example prompt
Why was it a dismal time? Why did you hate being there?	Choose one of these or your own: ■ It was dismal because I was bored all the time. ■ I found it dismal having only my granddad to talk to.
How do you think Darryl felt about not being believed? Do you think he might have regretted anything he'd done before?	How do you think he felt? ■ Angry that people did not trust him. ■ Annoyed with himself for lying in the past. Your own ideas?
Let's use some adverbs to describe how they fought. Fill in the words: Jason tried_____ to distract him, but the dragon _____ly used his strength to get past. Jason stabbed his sword _____ly into the dragon's nearest side.	Improve the fight by using one of these or your own: ■ The dragon's tail lashed viciously, cutting Jason's flesh. ■ Jason bravely lunged at the dragon, thrusting his sword fiercely into its side.
What kind of monster was he? Change bad for a word which makes him sound more scary. Write it in the box.	Try one of these or your own instead of bad: ■ ferocious ■ terrifying ■ evil
What type of boy is James? Good, bad, kind, shy, excitable, loud, naughty? Try to help us **know** him. James was a	Describe James's character. Perhaps: ■ James was a kind, likeable boy with a great sense of humour. For instance.... ■ James was often excitable and noisy but would be quiet and serious when he was working.
What do you think the merman said to the mermaid before they went home together?	Write one of these or your own ending: ■ 'I love you' said the merman. The mermaid took his hand and they swam away. ■ The merman looked embarrassed as he explained to the mermaid why he had taken so long to find her. She forgave him with a smile.

A Chimpanzee (Above-average Y4)

Learning intention: To write an effective description.

A chimpanzee

A chimpanzee baby does learn from it mother. A chimpanzee can crack nuts with a stone and can dig out termite nest and fashion twigs. The size of the mother is quite big a baby chimp is small. The colour of both of the chimps are black. The shape of the mother is big and tall a baby chimp is small and cuddly. A chimp is a very

What are their faces like? How do they look standing up? How do they walk?

clever animal and it they both come from the monkey family. The chimps like swinging on branches. The noise the make is oo aah. A monkeys face is like a humans face. The chimp stands up on two feet. Sometimes chimps walk mostly they swing to branches.

Black Beauty (Above-average Y6)

Learning intention: To write a given story from the point of view of one of the characters.

Black Beauty

"He is a good man, master, to everyone ecxept me.
He picks on me if the ground isn't crushed enough.
Always is he talking kindly, but to me he uses a rough and tuff voice."

Black Beauty - or so I call her, her mother loves him to bits she is always following him. She is his favourite

I'm a ploughboy and my name is Dick.
I pick blackberries and throw what I don't want. at the horses I also throw sticks and stones at the horses to amuse me.

One day I was throwing things at the horses, but I didn't see Master in the next field.
I heard a clatter over by the pence and thought it was the horses but it was master.
I didn't see him but he was shouting and shouting and then out of know where he shouted
"What do you think you are doing! he blared out.

What did you say to try to defend or explain your actions?

I should of known that you were hurting them you, you horrid boy," roared Master. He clouted me around the ears and told me that my service was needed nomore.
"Take your money and go" he shouted.
Just thinking about it makes my ears sting. I still visit in the far corner but not for long.

PTO.

The new man who looked after the horses. was called Daniel. He's always working and Master thinks he's the best ploughboy he's ever had. Daniel does take care of the horses. The horses like him alot so I suppose he is alright."   Good work

(continued)

Black Beauty.

(84)

*   "I should have known that you were hurting the horses you, you horrid little boy" he roared.
   "But, but I... umm," I mumbled.
"But what. You were hurting the horses and thats final...
   "But."
   "Don't say a word your services are needed nomore. It doesn't take alot to get hire a new plough boy!"

Return Journey of Jason (Average Y5)

Learning intention: To use adjectives and adverbs.

Return Journey of Jason

After Jason retrieved the Golden Fleece, he and his Argonauts sailed for home.

There was a jagged, black, dirty, ~~enormous~~ rock they were heading ~~towards~~ towards. ~~to then.~~ Suddenly it ~~and~~ made an enormous hole in the middle of the boat. One of the Argonauts tried to mend the hole. Along came a fierce, slimy, scally dragon that lept at the Argonauts and Jason. Jason was ready to fight the dragon the dragon blew icy, cold freezing water. He told the dragon to follow him and see who wins the golden fleece.

So the dragon went with them. *

Some good description and an adverb. Well done.

* Lets use adverbs and adjectives to describe the fight.
Finish off my sentence. Write another yourself.

The dragon's sharp, scaly tail lashed viciously cutting fearsly into Jason's red flesh.
Jason raised his sword and cut the dragon in half

lovely!

You're in charge! (Above-average Y6)

Learning intention: To write a story with an effective beginning, middle and ending.

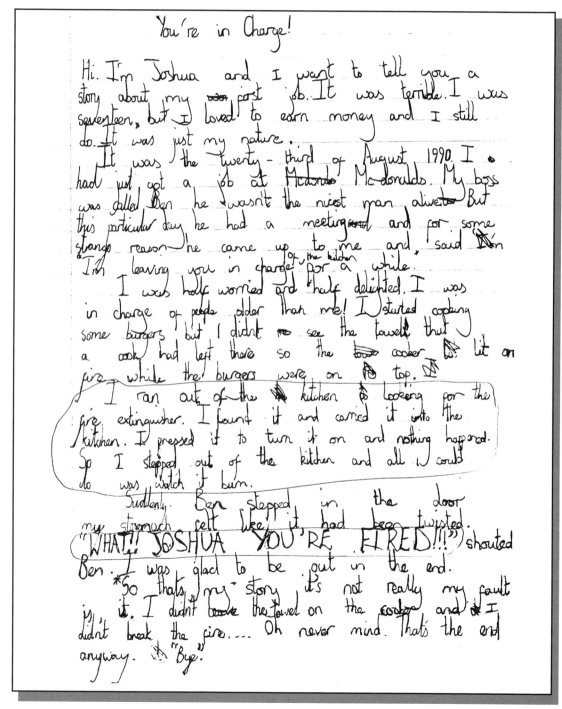

(continued)

Would you improve your ending. If you think seriously about the ending I'm sure you could make the final paragraph much more interesting - perhaps with a warning to other people - what did you learn?

* So the Point of that? It's what I'm hearing all over the place. There's a few all to do with fire safety. First, is that you should never leave a towel on a cooker, secondly, look around before you turn on oven on and finally always have a working fire extinguisher in a room. So there you have it. I could have sued but I just went home and cried like a girl.

Cinderella: the ending (Average Y6)

Learning intention: To write a non-boring ending, thinking especially about adverbs, adjectives and powerful words.

Cinderella:
the ending.

L.O: To Write a "non-boring" ending, thinking especially about adverbs, adjectives & powerful Verbs

Cinderella Was in the Corner, Waiting to try the Slipper on. The Prince impatiently called her over. She Was Very nervous. Cinderella Walked slolwly, half way over to the prince. "Come on dear We haVent got all day," Said the prince aiming the Words to her only, like a bullet. Hearing this, Cinderella Went pale and got more nervous than eVer. She Walked over the rest of the Way to him and stuck her Stinky foot out for the prince. It Was a perfect fit. The ugly Sisters Were Jealous. Dandini told the prince that the Wedding Would take place in a Week, and that everyone Was inVited (apart from the ugly Sisters of Course) So They liVed happilly eVer after.
  I'm sure the Ugly sisters were jealous but can you find a more exciting way of expressing this Bernardo?
The ugly Sisters Were green With enVy, their Spots exploded from the rage.

The impact of quality marking

Many teachers report of the outstanding progress children make when they are focused on success and improvement. One teacher sent me an exercise book from one of her children to show the development. Figures 6 and 7 show before and after samples of her development during the course of Year 2.

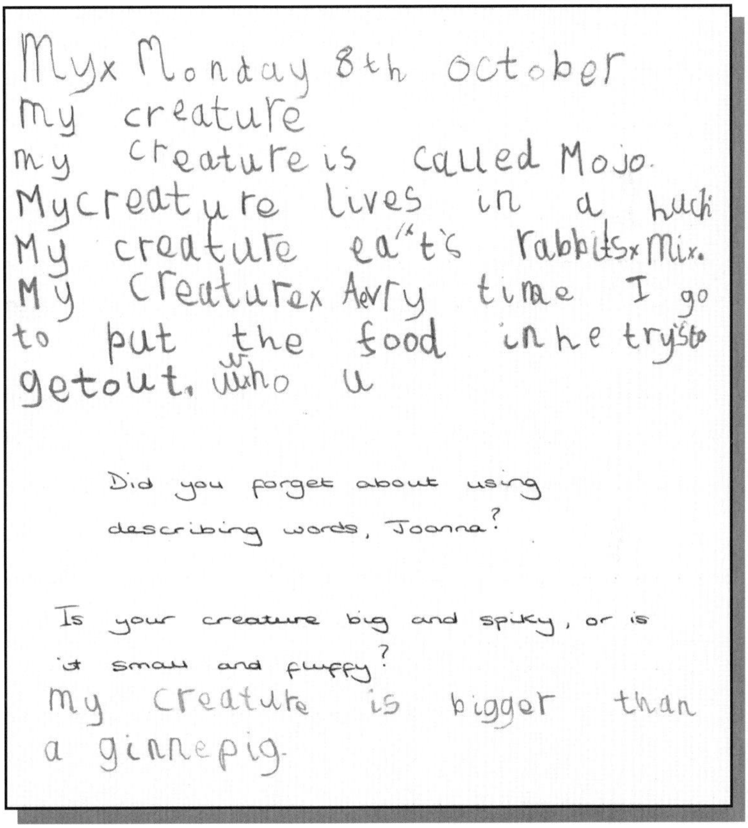

Myx Monday 8th october
my creature
my creature is called Mojo.
Mycreature lives in a huch
My creature ea"t's rabbits×Mix.
My creaturex Avry time I go
to put the food in he tryst
getout, who u

Did you forget about using
describing words, Joanna?

Is your creature big and spiky, or is
it small and fluffy?
my creature is bigger than
a ginnepig.

Fig. 6 (8th October)

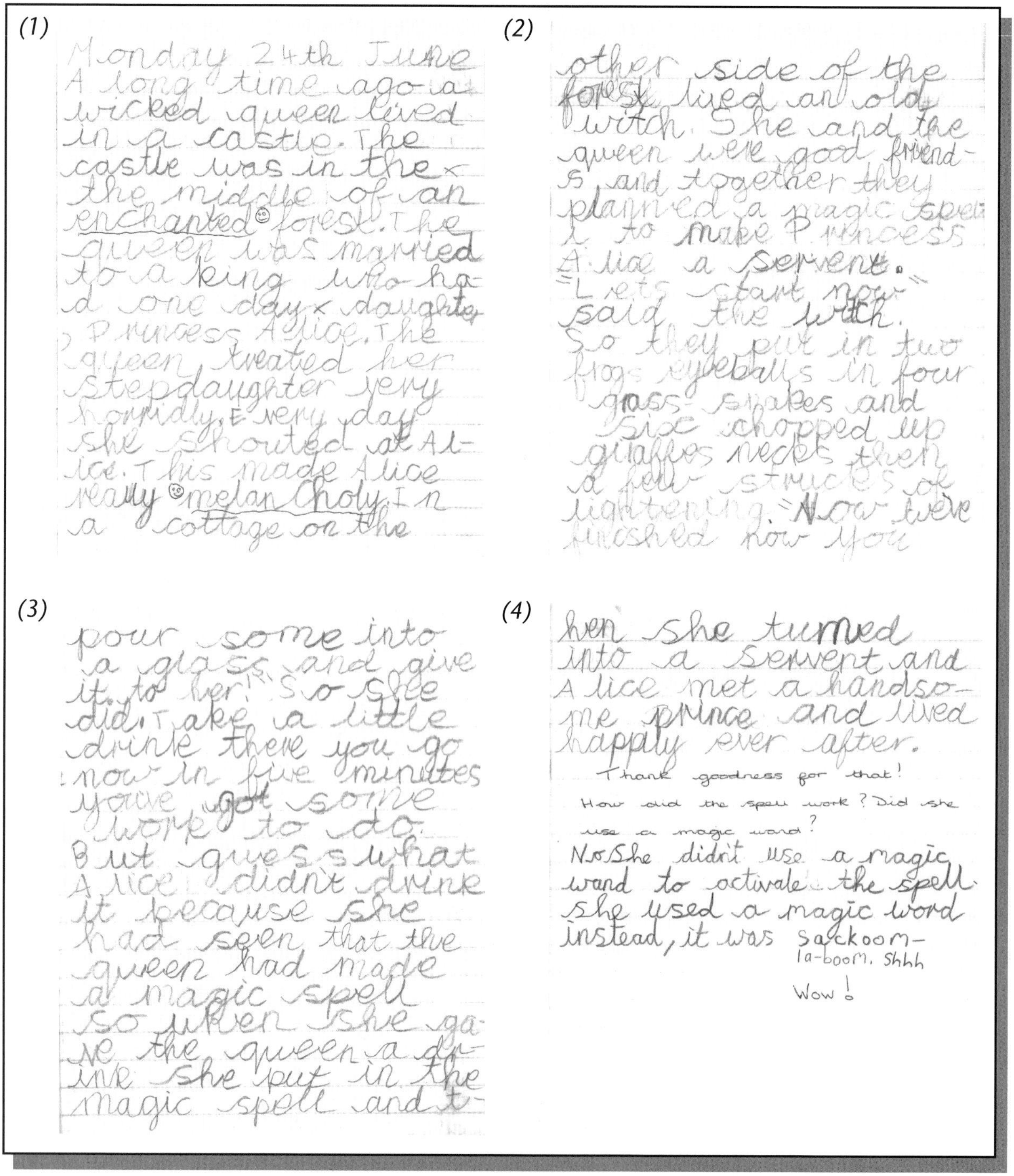

(1)

Monday 24th June
A long time ago a
wicked queen lived
in a castle. The
castle was in the
the middle of an
enchanted forest. The
queen was married
to a king who had
one day daughter
Princess Alice. The
queen treated her
stepdaughter very
horridly. Every day
she shouted at Al-
ice. This made Alice
really melancholy. In
a cottage on the

(2)

other side of the
forest lived an old
witch. She and the
queen were good friend-
s and together they
planned a magic spell
to make Princess
Alice a servent.
"Lets start now"
said the witch.
So they put in two
frogs eyeballs in four
grass snakes and
five chopped up
giraffes necks then
a few strikes of
lightening. "Now we're
finished now you

(3)

pour some into
a glass and give
it to her." So she
did. Take a little
drink there you go
now in five minutes
you've got some
work to do.
But guess what
Alice didn't drink
it because she
had seen that the
queen had made
a magic spell
So when she ga-
ve the queen a dr-
ink she put in the
magic spell and t-

(4)

hen she turned
into a servent and
Alice met a handso-
me prince and lived
happily ever after.
Thank goodness for that!
How did the spell work? Did she
use a magic word?
No She didn't use a magic
wand to activate the spell
she used a magic word
instead, it was sackoom-
la-boom. Shhh
Wow!

Fig. 7 The same child's writing, eight months later

After only five weeks of trialling quality marking, the Gillingham findings were as follows:

Teachers' views

(a) Impact on children's writing

■ Many teachers had noticed an improvement in children's writing.

■ Teachers reported that children were *'coming up with good additions'* because of the prompts; story openings had improved; there was more 'colour' in the work.

(b) Impact on children's attitudes towards writing

■ Some teachers had noticed that children had accepted the strategy as a structured classroom routine, a way in which to help them improve:

'This way of working makes more of a continuum of learning for a child. Takes away the idea of closed, "finished with" set of fragmented tasks. Much more developmental. There is definitely less "coasting" from children. Even with the weaker ones – they are encouraged to think "This is where I am on my learning path" NOT "I'm never going to get anywhere" because everyone is making improvements as part of the classroom routine.' (Y2 teacher)

'Yes, it has improved their work. It has given a framework where the children feel safe. Everyone gets three highlights, everyone has one thing to improve. They share and talk about what they have to do. It is the same for all children.' (Y6 teacher)

■ The routine of highlighting was reported as underpinning a new confidence in children:

'When they see their successes, it makes them more confident to tackle the bits that were not so successful.' (Y4 teacher)

'They're willing to carry on and write a bit more.' (Y2 teacher)

'Low self-esteem is raised by the highlighting. I'm really pleased. One of my very least able children who used to always say "This is no good – this is all wrong" now sometimes comes up with his work and says "I think you'll find something good in this".' (Y6 teacher)

(c) Impact on children's reflection about their writing

■ A few teachers reported that having to make improvements had prompted children to 'think more about how to improve':

'They are reflecting in a way they haven't done before.' (Y3/4 teacher)

'It makes them think about re-editing their work.' (Y5 teacher)

(d) Impact on children's learning about writing

■ Some Key Stage 2 teachers reported that children were learning from responding to the prompts and were seeing that they could transfer successful improvements into subsequent pieces of work:

'They take note of your comments – it kind of affirms for them something they can do: "Oh I did that improvement so I'm gonna do it again in another bit of writing".' (Y5 teacher)

'They are becoming more aware of what "good" writing' is.' (Y3 teacher)

Children's views

Most of the children were in favour of the distance-marking strategy for the following reasons:

(a) Having the highlights was a boost

'It's a better way of marking. This shows what interesting stuff you've done.' (Average Y4)

'It makes you feel like you've done it well this time.' (Above-average Y3)

'I know where I did well and I feel cheerful that I did something well.' (Below-average Y6)

(b) The highlights and improvements offered an opportunity for self-evaluation

'I can learn from my mistakes and I can look back and see what sort of things I've done and how I've done it.' (Average Y5)

'It helps me to think "well I've really done well here but not so well here". You know what you need to improve.'
(Above-average Y6)

(c) The prompts offered a welcome mechanism for improvement

'It shows me the weaknesses of my writing and I can improve on them.' (Above-average Y6)

'I really think it has improved my writing because now we can improve it whereas before she didn't ask us to improve it. She didn't tell us how to make it better.' (Average Y3)

(d) There were clear benefits in *writing down* improvements

(i) it forced you to act:
'It makes you do something about improving.'
'You don't really pay attention [to feedback] if it isn't written.'

(ii) it encouraged further thinking about how to make an improvement:
'Writing it down gives me more understanding.'
'Because it gets my brain working and I write more.'
'It gives you the chance to think it through.'
'It's better than the teacher writing it, it makes you think for yourself.'

(iii) it proved to the teacher you could do it:
'So he can see that we've improved. We could be lying and say "I thought of it". It is forever and I can read it again.'
'So the teacher sees we know how to improve.'
'I want the teacher to know what I mean.'
'So she knows we can and we know how to.'

(iv) it acted as an aide-memoire:
'By writing it, you don't forget it.'
'So you remember to improve on that.'

'I can read it over and over and probably understand it more.'
'Even though the improvement takes up more time, you know what you're doing, whereas if you just think it, you lose it straight away.'

(v) written improvements provided a record for reference:
'You can look back on it before the next story.'
'I try to use the ideas next time.'

(e) They had learnt from the highlights and type of improvements they had been asked to make and were applying this in new contexts

'I change words for better words now.'
'People can now get the idea of what I see and what ideas I have.'
'Normally teachers just tick it. Miss M highlights and you know what she likes so next time you can use the same thing in a different way, or use that word again.'

Impact on teachers and teaching

The majority of teachers (87%) said that the strategy had been instrumental in influencing their practice:

■ The biggest impact on teaching was that teachers were **more conscious about narrowing their 'marking eye'** so as to give written feedback only on the learning intention and the success criteria.

'I feel more focus and I'm more inclined to make my comments relevant to the learning intention. It keeps me from getting carried away by spellings and handwriting.' (Y6 teacher)

'In a way I am more aware of what I'm marking for. Before I used to mark everything and I sometimes lost the point of the exercise.' (Y3 teacher)

■ Similarly, with Reception and Year 1 teachers the biggest impact had been raised consciousness about **the importance of making oral feedback relate to success criteria.**

■ Teachers reported that they were **generally more positive and upbeat about learning,** *'looking for more things that were good and not negative'.*

'I've changed my culture of marking from all wrong to making it better.' (Y6 teacher)

'A whole shift in my marking orientation – now looking for what children have done well – before I tended to look for what they had done wrong.' (Y4 teacher)

'Its changed my language when speaking with the children, I'm more positive.' (Reception teacher)

■ Importantly, several teachers reported that the strategy had prompted them to **have more empathy with the learners and consider the learner** when giving feedback.

'It's made me very aware of the pointlessness of just saying "Well done". You need to write something relevant.' (Y4 teacher)

'It made me feel very guilty to just put "Good". I see the power of putting a comment rather than something that doesn't tell them anything.' (Y3/4 teacher)

'I appreciate how much work has to be done to do a story, now. It is not just WHAT is a story but HOW.' (Y3 teacher)

'It is forcing me to focus on each individual and where they're at in their learning.' (Y6 teacher)

Key principles

■ Quality feedback using the success and improvement model is usually more appropriate with specific learning intentions.

■ It can be useful to focus on improvements for applications occasionally.

■ Improvement prompts tend to be: elaborating and extending, adding a word or sentence, changing the text, or justifying.

■ Teachers' prompts tend to be *reminder, scaffolded* or *example.*

■ The strategy works in all areas, but highlights are irrelevant with closed exercises.

■ Place yourself in the shoes of the child when considering how they answer the questions.

■ Teachers and children found benefits in using this form of marking and children's writing improved.

■ Learning intentions are more manageable if abbreviated as the title of the work.

■ Individual targets are often unmanageable.

INSET ideas

1. Introduce teachers to the success and improvement model, stressing that they would only mark occasional pieces in this way (once a week, twice at the most). Show some of the examples in this chapter.
2. Use the same piece of a child's writing for a whole staff to mark using the strategy. Get people to share their improvement suggestions. Encourage them to go beyond a reminder prompt!
3. At a subsequent meeting, teachers can bring children's writing and have a go at the strategy in pairs, again reading out their improvement suggestions to each other.
4. Give teachers copies of the 'Improvement prompts' grid from the *Enriching Feedback* page of the Hodder website (see p. viii), to provide guidance when they are coming up with improvement suggestions.
5. After introducing the strategy to their class (using an OHP) they could give the children their work back that was marked in this way (after one or two were marked in the staff meeting).
6. Teachers bring along to the next meeting the children's work, now complete with improvements! They each give feedback about the impact and what they learnt from this first round of marking and improvement.
7. Try the strategy out in staff meetings with other subjects.

9

Self- and paired marking

'Independent learners have the ability to seek out and gain new skills, new knowledge and new understandings. They are able to engage in self-reflection and to identify the next steps in their learning. Teachers should equip learners with the desire and the capacity to take charge of their learning through developing the skills of self-assessment.'

(Assessment Reform Group, 2002)

Our aim is, of course, to involve children as far as possible in the analysis and constructive criticism of their own work. We want them to use self-evaluation continually, so that reflection, pride in successes, modification and improvement become a natural part of the process of learning. Many teachers who have been using formative assessment for some time talk about the integration of what used to be ends of lessons or work marked away from the child into the actual structure of a lesson. Time is built-in for reflection in structured ways (e.g. *'Find one word you are really proud of and underline it. Tell the person next to you'/ 'Three minutes to identify two places you think you have done this well and read it to your partner'.* After whole-class sharing for a minute or two... *'Five minutes to find one place you could improve. Write your improvement at the bottom of your work...').* If the teacher is the only person giving feedback, the balance is wrong and the children become powerless in having any stake in their learning. What is more, marking will be, in those circumstances, time-consuming, unwieldy and 'end-on'.

Self-marking

Closed exercises

Self-marking of closed exercises has been discussed earlier in this book (see page 70). If the teacher goes through the answers and the processes involved with the class, learning is likely to be enhanced. Getting children to mark each other's closed exercises is mostly counter-productive, because they do not have access to their own work as the problems are being discussed.

Checking work

Linda Stibbons, from the Pupil Achievement Unit in Leeds, has introduced the 'green pencil' approach to encourage children to routinely 'check' their own work. Children are asked to put down their pens and pick up a special green pencil for the last few minutes of the lesson. She says:

> *There could be a whole-class checking, an improvement focus relating to one of the success criteria or it could be an ongoing check on sentence demarcation, key spellings, adjectives, etc. If there are group or individual targets, then it might be appropriate to check against those. This provides time for children to read their work and an opportunity for the teacher to praise their improvements. This helps to establish the culture of 'safe to have a go' and 'I am always the first reader of my own writing' as well as raising self-esteem.*

Teachers in Leeds using this approach have found that more learning takes place in the two minutes' checking time than if children are given that time to continue their work.

When asking children to check for spellings, it is more productive to ask them to look at spellings which *they know are wrong* rather than those for which they have no idea.

Quality self-marking

Quality self-marking is clearly very powerful, but needs a gradual training programme to be successful. If children are let loose on their own or each other's work too soon, they can head mercilessly for the spelling errors or make stinging remarks about the quality of the handwriting or work in general.

The first stage of shifting power from teacher to child is to get children to mark their own work. I lead on to response partner work later, but this involves the emotional dynamic between two children, so should be tackled after children are confident about reflecting on their own work first.

Stage 1: children identify their successes

Teachers using the success and improvement model have found that children as young as Year 2 can easily identify their own successes if the learning intention is clear (a knowledge, skill or concept rather than a broad application). These can then be read to the person next to them or shared in a group or whole-class setting. The positive influence of identifying successes has a great impact on children's self-esteem and motivation to continue to improve their work.

Stage 2: children identify a place for improvement

Once the finding of successes is established, children can be asked – after they have been working for some time – to not only identify one or two successes, but also to find one place in their work which could be improved against the learning intention. One strategy is to ask children to identify this place by drawing a wiggly line underneath the sentence or phrase to be improved, ready for the teacher to write an improvement suggestion. The teacher then writes the improvement suggestion for the child.

Stage 3: children identify their successes and make an 'on the spot' improvement

Children can then be asked to identify an area to be improved and make the improvement as part of the lesson.

It seems to work best if children do this first on their own, although, if children are used to paired discussion, they might well be able to launch headlong into paired discussion about the best ways of improving something.

Once this stage has been reached, the teacher's role changes from being a full-time 'marker' to an effective interventionist, commenting on children's efforts and getting involved in their decision making.

Many of the pieces analysed in the previous chapter included elements marked by the child. Figure 8 shows an entire piece marked by a Year 6 child: the child has changed the length of the track and changed batteries to cells.

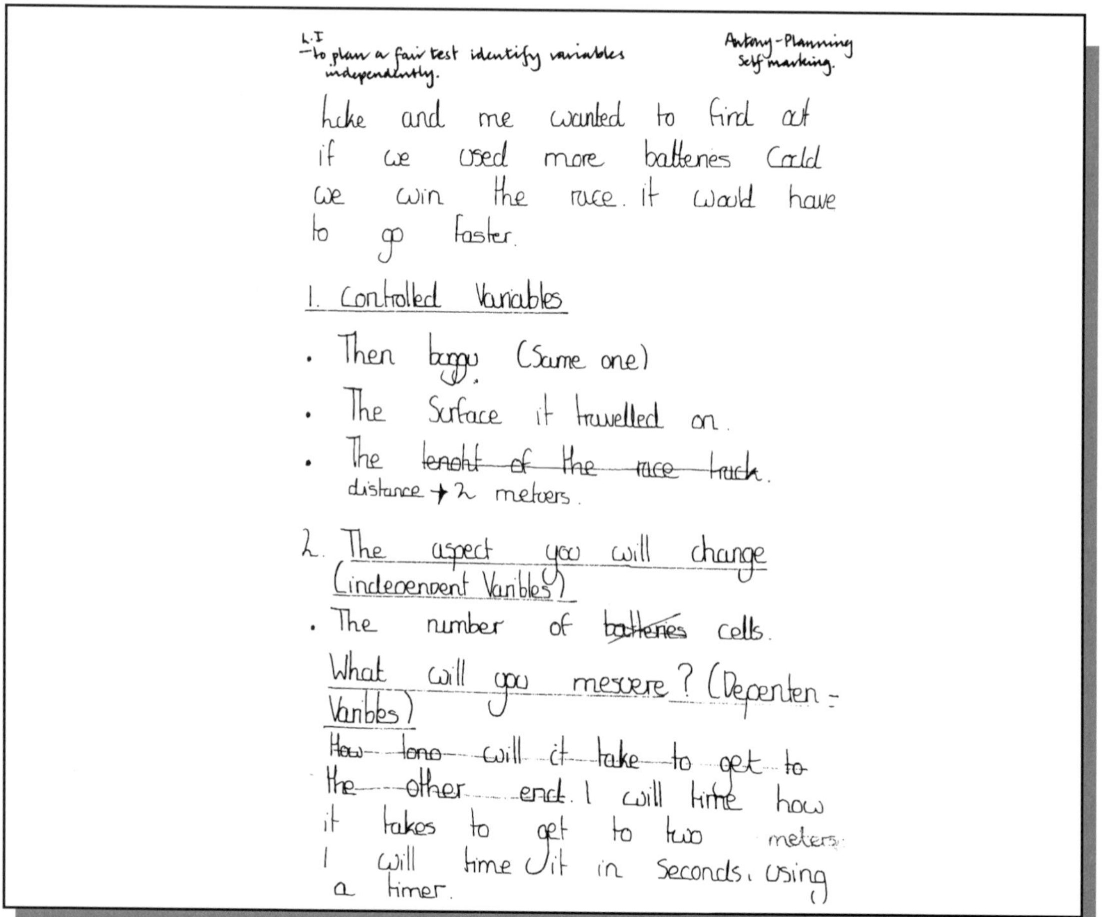
L.I
– to plan a fair test identify variables independantly.

Antony – Planning
Self marking.

Luke and me wanted to find out if we used more batteries could we win the race. it would have to go faster.

1. Controlled Variables
- Then buggy (Same one)
- The Surface it travelled on.
- The ~~lenght of the race track~~.
  distance + 2 meters.

2. The aspect you will change (indeoendent Varibles)
- The number of ~~batteries~~ cells.

What will you mesere? (Depenten-Varibles)
~~How long will it take to get to the other end.~~ I will time how it takes to get to two meters. I will time it in seconds. using a timer.

Fig. 8

Quality paired marking

Findings from Gillingham

Year 2 to Year 6 Gillingham teachers were invited to experiment by asking children to highlight success in a partner's work. Many teachers were already asking children to comment on each other's work through 'response partners' or 'buddy checkers':

'I have introduced writing journals, for children to write to a friend and share a comment about one thing that they liked about their friend's writing.' (Y2 teacher)

'I don't exactly ask them to "highlight" success with a pen. What I do is ask them to work in pairs, read each other's work – then say two positive things and make one suggestion for improvement.' (Y4 teacher)

The general feeling from those teachers was that although children could say 'good things' about another's work, they would need support to be able to relate those good things specifically to the learning intention or success criteria of the lesson. Children really need to understand what success would look like before they critique a friend's work.

A few teachers reported that what transpired in one or two Key Stage 2 classrooms was that children wanted to discuss the highlights with their friends and were doing it at their own instigation:

'They started to do it themselves. They look at the highlights and discuss. They are naturally doing it.' (Y6 teacher)

A small number of teachers who had tried peer highlighting had found that some children (as young as Year 2) were able to spot the appropriate bits to highlight:

'When they are working with partners they can pick out the bits they think are best and know why. A child will say "That's what we had to do – these are the best bits."' (Y2 teacher)

'Sometimes they are able to say whether work met the success criteria – and say why.' (Y3 teacher)

Impact, in some cases, may have been due to allowing time for children to consider the marking, as some teachers did:

'I have given them time to share their highlighted bits with each other – this made an impact on the use of conjunctions when that was the learning intention – some children could see from others' highlights how to use conjunctions.' (Y6 teacher)

'Children do understand the prompts better when they can discuss them with a friend.' (Y6 teacher)

'I am consciously making time for them to talk about their improvement.' (Y5 teacher).

'I ask them as a matter of course to read the highlights to themselves and think them over.' (Y4 teacher)

The emotional impact of paired marking

Many teachers get children to work with a 'response partner'. This can involve a few minutes of helping each other to improve their work or a more lengthy process of reading whole pieces and analysing them more fully together.

In order to fully understand the emotional impact of sharing one's work with a peer and receiving criticism, no matter how constructive, I ask teachers on my courses to engage in a writing activity and some collaborative marking (see the INSET ideas at the end of this chapter). The experience is always illuminating for teachers. To begin with, they usually experience some form of anxiety about being judged by a peer, and things like who reads the work first and holding eye contact are highly significant to them. Body language and tone of voice become areas of sensitivity and the importance of receiving some positive comments first are highlighted.

The table shows which aspects of body language and verbal language were identified by the participants of one course as having either a positive or negative impact on them while they were engaged in the process of paired marking.

Body language of the response partner:		Verbal language of the response partner:	
Positive	**Negative**	**Positive**	**Negative**
Moving in to look at the work and out when the partner was talking	Avoiding eye contact	Praise	Silences could be positive if encouraging the author to speak, or negative if waiting for the response partner to 'pass judgement'
Smiling	No smiling	Appropriate laughter	No appreciation
Nodding	Foot tapping	Clarification questions	Jumping to conclusions
Holding eye contact	Playing with pens	Empathy over the task	Clipped approach
Hand waving when making a point	Sitting on hands	Reassuring words used	
Facing and mirroring		References to the criteria of the task	
Looking intently at the work			
Pointing to the work			

As a result of various sessions of this kind, the following 'Golden rules' are suggested when embarking on paired marking.

Golden rules for children marking with a response partner

1 Both partners should be roughly the same ability, or just one jump ahead or behind, rather than a wide gap.

2 The pupil needs time to reflect on and check his or her writing before a response partner sees it.

3   The response partner should begin with a positive comment about the work.

4   The roles of both parties need to be clearly defined.

5   The response partner needs time to take in the child's work, so it is best for the author to read the work out first. This also establishes ownership of the piece.

6   Children need to be trained in the success and improvement process, or whatever is being used, so that they are confident with the steps involved.

7   Children must both agree the part to be changed.

8   The author should make the marks on his or her work, as a result of the paired discussion.

9   Children need to be reminded that the focus of their task is the learning intention.

10   The response partner should ask for clarification rather than jump to conclusions.

11   The improvement suggestions should be verbal and not written down. The only writing necessary would be the identification of successes and the improvement itself.

12   It would be useful to role-play response partners in front of the class, perhaps showing them the wrong way and the right way over a piece of work.

13   It could be useful to do this two-thirds of the way through a lesson, so that children can make the improvement and continue writing with a better understanding of quality.

Figure 9 shows some science work carried out by a Year 6 child who worked with a response partner. At the beginning of the year, the teacher had marked their work exclusively. By the spring term, the children were able to operate entirely independently in a paired marking situation.

How will we keep our drink cold?

- to investigate which materials are best for keeping our drink cool. (Thermal insulators)

- to draw conclusions from our results.

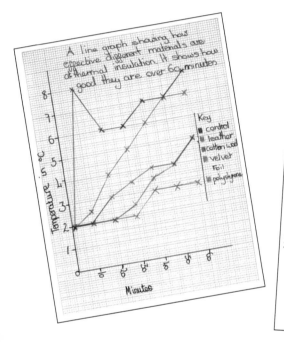

A line graph showing how effective different materials are at thermal insulation. It shows how good they are over 60 minutes

Key
- control
- leather
- cotton wool
- velvet
- Foil
- polystyrene

Temperature °C

Minutes

Not much change? Look at your lines or your graph - follow along the line and tell the story of the line. When does it show a rise in temperature? Is it rising fast

Conclusion

We found that after ten minutes polystyrene, foil, leather and cotton-wool were the best thermal insulators all at 2°C I was suprized the drink with no material over it (control) was far warmer than the covered drinks. I thought leather would be the worst thermal insulator but it was only 0.5°C warmer than the other drinks. I think this had something to do with the out-side temperature, It was a warm environment, so clearly the materials we choose to insulate must have protected them from the heat. There was not much change in results after 20 minutes; foil, velvet and polystyrene had not changed from the beginning. The control was now 6°C. The other liquids rose in temperature by 1 or 2 °C I expected a major change in results and I also expected the liquids to rise in temperature every 10 minutes. After

30 minutes there was hardly any change. When we took the reading for cotton-wool we could not decide on a reading, some said it was 3.4°C and some said it was 3.5°C. It took a while but finnally we decided on 3.5°C. In my opinion it was 3.4°C. Even though there wasnt much difference I still think that it wasnt accurate In 40, 50 and 60°C there wasn't much change in results. On the whole foil and polystyrene were the best. It was a fair experiment, but not very accurate.

Miss I used a not situation from my other experiment.

Fig. 9

(continued)

Con. and insulating material	Temperature after						
	0 min	10 min	20 min	30 min	40 min	50 min	60 min
Control	2°C	8°C	6°C	6°C	7°C	7°C	8°C
Cotton wool	2°C	2°C	3°C	3·5°C	4°C	4°C	5°C
Foil	2°C	2°C	2°C	2°C	3°C	3°C	3°C
leather	2°C	2·5°C	4°C	5°C	6°C	7°C	7°C
Velvet	2°C	2°C	2°C	2·5°C	3·5°C	4°C	5°C
Polystyrene	2°C	2°C	2°C	2°C	3°C	3°C	3°C

Closing the gap Response.

Although there was no change in results for foil, polystyrene and velvet at 20 minutes cotton-wool's and leather's results were already suggesting that they weren't the best insulating materials as the temperature was rising—In fact 'leather' continued to rise steadily in temperature during the whole investigation until the last 10 minutes where it appears to have reached a more constant temperature. Although the cotton-wool also rose in temperature the increase wasn't so great and so it must be a better insulator than leather.

Carolyn Lyndsay, the teacher of this class, explains now how her feedback moved towards self- and paired marking and includes illustrative children's views. I have also included here (Figure 10) this teacher's poster of the rules agreed by the class about marking.

Fig. 10

I have found that, as children continue to experience this form of feedback, they begin to decide their level of response, not in a cheeky way, but in a far more self-determining way. Sometimes they will just respond and other times they will take it one step further than you, the marker, expected. I have also noticed that, as self- and paired marking gets going, children are far more likely to not just discuss the teacher's feedback, but also they now discuss with each other (and sometimes me) how to respond and I find they take on board each other's suggestions regarding how to take the response further than the 'closing the gap' question requires. Furthermore, children are far more

(continued)

likely to question your highlighting, having been involved in the marking process themselves. They now want to understand your thinking behind the marking, again not in a cheeky way, but more in a relationship sort of way – it also serves to make all those in the marking process feel far more valued. Children's comments:

> 'On Tuesday we started to self-mark our own work. I think this is great, I was able to show everyone what was good and how I improved my work. I think sometimes it might be a good leave the response to the next day. You see things you hadn't before. But sometimes you need to do it then, it sort of depends.'

> '. . . at first I didn't mind highlighting Charlotte's work, but I didn't want to suggest how she could make it better. I really like Charlotte, and want to be her friend, but then Charlotte said I hadn't told her how to improve. We talked together and worked on a question for her to respond to. I think this was good so that next time I sort of know what to do and if I'm stuck I can just ask them to work with me . . .'

This has frequently been the case . . . I have found that, by introducing self-marking first, children have a structure and process they can fall back on when they move on to paired marking.

> 'I know that place value is important in decimals, but I can't understand what happens after the hundredths. Miss will need to do more on them, because I think I need just a bit more. I'll put it on a post-it so that she can do something about it.'

I have a system that, as well as circle time, where we raise issues, we also have a post-it board where children can jot down issues and requests . . . we then collectively decide who has to deal with them . . . them, me, us, other adults, school council, parents reps, whoever – hence Rosie's post-it plea.

> 'I enjoyed helping Kieron on Wednesday. But we didn't agree on the second highlight, so we had to go back to the learning intention and success criteria and really work on them . . . I didn't think they were very good. There was too much in them. Me and Kieron decided on a bit of the learning intention. He said it was the bit he wasn't good at and we then used that for the 'closing the gap' question. I helped him with that. He then looked at mine and it surprised me the bit he asked me to improve, but that's because he was seeing it from the outside, I think that was good.'

(continued)

'I'm still not sure after I have done the first part of the sum if I need to round my answer up or down if it's a word question. I need to get help with this.'

'I knew there was something about my second paragraph in the History so I got Adebola to work with me. Adebola said she couldn't understand it so she asked me to show her the planning and we went to the second paragraph. She asked me to write three bullet points under the heading, then to write a sentence about each bullet point. This was a good idea and I was able to use some of my sentences from the paragraph. I think the report is much better now.'

'Sam's comment in the Spelling Log gave me a new way of remembering those types of words . . . so I gave him one of my ways.'

Our Agreement on Marking Partnerships

We decided that there were some rules we all needed to keep. When we become Marking Partners we all agree to . . .

- **respect** our partner's work because they have done their best and so their work should be valued.

- **try to see** how they have tackled the Learning Intention and only try to improve things that are to do with the learning intention.

- **tell** our partner the good things we see in their work.

- **listen** to our partner's advice because we are trying to help each other do better in our work.

- **look for** a way to help our partner to achieve the Learning Intention better by giving them a 'closing the gap' activity to do.

- try to make our suggestion as **clear** as possible.

- try to make our suggestions **positive**.

- get our partner to **talk about** what they tried to achieve in their work.

- **be fair** to our partner. We will not talk about their work behind their backs because we wouldn't like them to do it to us and it wouldn't be fair.

Key principles

■ Aim for children constructively marking their own work against the learning intention of the task, sometimes with a partner.

■ Children need to be trained, in stages, to mark their own and each others' work.

■ There need to be ground rules about paired marking to avoid anxiety.

INSET ideas

1. Share ideas about existing practice for self- and paired marking.
2. Build on this by asking teachers to trial asking children to find their own successes. Bring examples to a staff meeting and discuss findings.
3. Teachers can trial children discussing their successes first, then the next stages outlined in this chapter, until children gradually have more control.
4. Set up a staff meeting in which teachers write for four minutes about, say, their journey to school that morning, using a learning intention such as *'Use similes and/or metaphors to add interest and humour to an account'*. They then get into groups of three:

    Two teachers mark one of their pieces together while the third person observes silently, writing under the columns shown on page 137. They then move round one space, so that, after three goes, each person will have had their work marked cooperatively and each person will have been an observer. They each share their observation findings **at the end**. Ask each group to feed back to the whole staff their findings and recommendations for 'golden rules' for paired marking.

10 You've read the book – now what?

The question I get asked the most after training sessions is *'How am I going to take all of this back to school?'* There is no easy answer to this, but here are some strategies.

Take your time

Formative assessment often involves major changes in people's thinking and needs time to be trialled, discussed and created by schools. It would be better to wait two years until there is a serious commitment on the school development plan to formative assessment, than to try to do it in a couple of staff meetings.

Shared analysis

People say it takes two years to embed, and that is with lots of staff meetings. Ideally you should introduce aspects of feedback one at a time, allowing input, discussion and feedback staff meetings. Rather than simply asking teachers to trial strategies in the classroom, it is more enabling to first have staff meetings in which teachers practise the strategies together (see the INSET suggestions throughout this book). Without this practice and very important follow-up discussion, teachers can feel ill-equipped to introduce new ideas. On my training days, I input for half the time and get people to try things out in the other half. Sharing and analysing people's attempts at creating success criteria or making improvement prompts really moves people in their understanding. After two or three meetings like this, people feel much more confident in planning or implementing new elements of their practice alone.

The main teacher development model used in Japan is something called 'Lesson Study'. Teachers form groups of four or five and plan one or two lessons a year together in fine detail, meeting after school several times. They plan the questions carefully and decide the possible answers the children might have, and how the teacher will respond to them. One person from the team then carries out the lesson, with the others watching and taking notes. They analyse what happens at the end, modify the lesson accordingly and repeat it on another occasion. The point of this method is not to have a growing bank of perfect lessons, but to develop teachers' expertise in planning and carrying out any lesson, based on these powerful experiences. It is the process of discussion, observation, analysis and reflection that has a major influence on their personal development.

Since reading about lesson study in *The Teaching Gap* (Stigler and Hiebert, 1999) I have tried to follow the principles of this in my advice to teachers and in my Learning Teams throughout the country. The 'bottom-up' model is sorely needed in our schools, and schools have the power to follow at least the essence of 'lesson study' in how staff meetings are run. See my INSET suggestions at the end of each chapter for some practical ideas.

Build on existing practice

Any practical strategies outlined in this book are derived from teachers, and should be seen as another suggestion adding to the teacher's existing repertoire, rather than to replace it. Teachers need to be encouraged to be 'action researchers' trialling not only ideas from this book but their own ideas. The end result should be modified strategies, which schools and teachers have created for themselves, using books like this, and the other resources referenced here, as a resource.

Base decisions on research principles

The Key Principles given at the end of each chapter list the things that really matter. When deciding on action, take account of these principles rather than the practical strategies. If the strategies are trialled without the underlying principle being understood, teachers can use them superficially. It is better to present the research in each case and first ask teachers what they are already doing to fulfil those principles. The ideas in this book can then be given as some possible things to trial.

Don't go it alone

Grab any opportunity to form a network of schools in which the same element is being explored, so that teachers can be observed and strategies and findings can be shared. See my website (www.shirleyclarke-education.org) for regular updates on the findings of the various Learning Teams around the country.

Endnote

Teachers are rarely told how expert they have become. In my travels around the world I have been struck many times by how far we have come in the last 15 years. UK primary teachers have exceptional expertise, which is still developing and growing, in literacy and numeracy and in starting from learning intentions. They have access to wonderful resources and have considerably elevated their expectations of children.

What is now needed is high teacher morale, greater power and more professional confidence. The groundwork has been done. The ingredients are all there for teachers to now pay more attention to learning than coverage, to focusing on what works best for the learning rather than for accountability, to make lessons fit the *children's* learning needs rather than the needs of outside parties. Hopefully, this book will inspire teachers to grab their professional confidence with both hands.

References and further reading

AAIA (Association of Assessment Inspectors and Advisors) (2001) *Primary Assessment Practice: Evaluation and Development Materials* (www.aaia.org.uk)

Abbott, J. (1994) *Learning Makes Sense*, in Education 2000 conference papers.

Assessment Reform Group (2002) *Assessment for Learning: Ten Principles* (www.assessment-reform-group.org.uk)

Abrami, P., Chambers, B., Poulsen, C., De Simone, C., Dápollonia, S. and Howden, J. (1995) *Classroom Connections: understanding and using co-operative learning*, Toronto: Harcourt Brace, quoted from Carnell, E. (2000) 'Dialogue, discussion and feedback', in Askew, S. (Ed.) *Feedback for Learning*, RoutledgeFalmer.

Askew, S. and Lodge, C. (2000) 'Gifts, ping-pong and loops-linking feedback and learning', in Askew, S. (Ed.) *Feedback for Learning*, RoutledgeFalmer.

Ausubel, D. P., Novak, J. and Hanesian, H. (1978) *Educational Psychology: A Cognitive View*, 2nd edn, Holt Rinehart and Winston.

Black, P., Harrison, C., Lee, C. Marshall, B. and Wiliam, D. (2002) *Working Inside the Black Box*, Kings College, London (020 7836 5454 ext.3189).

Black, P. and Wiliam, D. (1998) 'Assessment and classroom learning', *Assessment in Education, 5*, 1.

Brooks, J.G. and Brooks, M.G. (1993) *In Search of Understanding: the case for constructivist classrooms*, Alexandria, VA, Association for Supervision and Curriculum Development.

Clarke, S. (1998) *Targeting Assessment in the Primary Classroom*, Hodder and Stoughton.

Clarke, S. (2001) *Unlocking Formative Assessment*, Hodder and Stoughton.

Connor, Colin (ed.) (1999) *Assessment in Action in the Primary School*, Falmer.

Craft, A. (1996) in MacGilchrist, B. (ed.) *Managing Access and Entitlement in Primary Education*, Routledge.

Crooks, T. (2001) Paper prepared for the 2001 Annual Meeting of the British Educational Research Association (BERA), Leeds, England, 13–15 September 2001 (in proceedings, but not presented because of travel delays caused by terrorist actions).

Dryden, G. and Vos, J. (2001) *The Learning Revolution*, Network Educational Press.

Dweck, C. (1986) 'Motivational processes affecting learning', *American Psychologist, 41*, 10, 1040–8.

Eppig, P. (1981) *Education by Design* – used in the UK as Critical Skills program by Success@Bristol (Bristol Education Action Zone).

Gardner, H. (1993) *Multiple Intelligence: The Theory in Practice*, Basic Books.

Gardner, H. (1983) *Frames of Mind*, Basic Books.

Gillingham Partnership website: www.gp4success.org

Hargreaves, E., McCallum, B. and Gipps, C. (2001) 'Teacher feedback strategies in primary classrooms-new evidence', in Askew, S. (ed.) *Feedback for Learning*, RoutledgeFalmer.

Hattie, J. (1992) 'Towards a model of schooling: a synthesis of meta-analyses', *Australian Journal of Education, 36*, 5–13.

OfSTED (1996) *General Report on Schools*, p.40, Office for Standards in Education.

QCA website: www.qca.org.uk for The LEARN Project and the Assessment for Learning site.

North Gillingham EAZ (DfES)/ Institute of Education (2001) Three Reports of the Gillingham Formative Assessment Project, www.gp4success.org

Robinson, K. (2000) AAIA (Assessment Advisors and Inspectors Association) Conference after-dinner speech.

Stevenson, H. W. and Stigler, J. W. (1992) *The Learning Gap*, Touchstone/Simon & Schuster.

Stigler, J.W. and Hiebert, J. (1999) *The Teaching Gap*, Free Press/Simon & Schuster.

Vygotsky, L. S. (1978) *Mind in Society*, Harvard University Press.

Ween, P., Winter, Jan, and Broadfoot, P. (2002) *Assessment: What's in it for schools?*, RoutledgeFalmer.